The Bible:
An Owner's Manual

The Bible:
An Owner's Manual

*What you need to know before
you buy and read your own Bible*

Robert R. Hann

Paulist Press · New York/Ramsey

Acknowledgements

The Publisher gratefully acknowledges the use of the following illustrations:

(p. vi) First page of the Book of Genesis from the *Berlin Guttenberg Bible.* Courtesy of The American Bible Society Library.

(p. 20) Translation of Psalm 98 © 1963 by The Grail, used by permission of Wm. Collins & Son Ltd. From *The Abbey Psalter* © 1981 by The Missionary Society of St. Paul the Apostle in the State of New York. Used by permission of Paulist Press.

(p. 80) First page of the Gospel of Matthew from the *Greek New Testament of Erasmus, 1516.* Courtesy of The American Bible Society Library.

Library of Congress
Catalog Card Number: 82-60750

ISBN: 0-8091-2503-X

Published by Paulist Press
545 Island Road, Ramsey, N.J. 07446

Printed and bound in the
United States of America

Contents

Incipit liber bresith que nos genesim
dicim9. In principio creauit deus celu
et terram. Terra autem erat inanis et
vacua: et tenebre erant sup facie abissi:
et sps dni ferebat sup aquas. Dixitq;
deus. Fiat lux. Et facta e lux. Et vidit
deus luce qp esset bona: et diuisit luce
a tenebris. appellauitq; luce diem et
tenebras nocte. Factuq; est vespe et
mane dies vnus. Dixit qp deus. Fiat
firmamentu in medio aquas: et diui
dat aquas ab aquis. Et fecit deus fir
mamentu: diuisitq; aquas que erat
sub firmameto ab hys q erant sup
firmamentu: et factu e ita. Vocauitq;
deus firmamentu celu: et factu e vespe
et mane dies secud9. Dixit vero deus.
Congregent aque que sub celo sut in
locu vnu et appareat arida. Et factu e
ita. Et vocauit deus aridam terram:
congregacionesq; aquap appellauit
maria. Et vidit deus qp esset bonu: et
ait. Germinet terra herba virente et
faciente semen: et lignu pomiferu faciens
fructu iuxta genus suu: cui9 semen in
semetipo sit sup terra. Et factu e ita. Et
protulit terra herba virente et faciente
seme iuxta genus suu: lignuq; faciens
fructu et habes vnuqdq; sementem scdm
specie sua. Et vidit deus qp esset bonu:
et factu est vespe et mane dies tercius.
Dixitq; aute deus. Fiant luminaria
in firmameto celi: et diuidat die ac
nocte: et sint in signa et tpa et dies et
annos: ut luceat in firmameto celi et
illuminet terra. Et factu e ita. Fecitq;
deus duo luminaria magna: lumiare
maius ut pesset diei et lumiare min9
ut pesset nocti et stellas: et posuit eas in
firmameto celi ut lucerent sup terra: et

pessent diei ac nocti: et diuiderent luce
ac tenebras. Et vidit de9 qp esset bonu:
et factu e vespe et mane dies quartus.
Dixit etia de9. Producat aque reptile
anime viuentis et volatile super terra
sub firmameto celi. Creauitq; deus cete
grandia: et omne aiam viuente atq;
motabile qua pduxerat aque i species
suas: et omne volatile scdm genus suu.
Et vidit deus qp esset bonu: benedixitq;
eis dicens. Crescite et multiplicamini: et
replete aquas maris: auesq; multipli
cent sup terra. Et factu e vespe et mane
dies quitus. Dixit quoq; deus. Pro
ducat terra aiam viuente in gene suo
iumenta et reptilia: et bestias terre scdm
species suas. Factuq; e ita. Et fecit de9
bestias terre iuxta species suas: iumen
ta et omne reptile terre i genere suo. Et
vidit deus qp esset bonu: et ait. Facia
mus hoiem ad ymagine et similitudine
nostra: et psit piscib9 maris: et vola
tilib9 celi et bestijs vniuseq; terre: omiq;
reptili qd mouetur i terra. Et creauit
deus hoiem ad ymagine et similitudine
sua: ad ymagine dei creauit illu: ma
sculu et femina creauit eos. Benedixit
q; illis deus: et ait. Crescite et multiplica
mini et replete terra: et sbicite ea: et dua
mini piscib9 maris: et volatilib9 celi:
et vniuersis animatibz que mouent
sup terra. Dixitq; de9. Ecce dedi vobis
omne herba afferente seme sup terra:
et vniusa ligna que hut in semetipis
semete genis sui: ut sint vobis i esca
et cuctis aiantibz terre: oniq; voluceri
celi et vniuersis q mouetur in terra: et
quibz est anima viues: ut habeat ad
vescendu. Et factu est ita. Vidit q; deus
cuncta que fecerat: et erant valde bona.

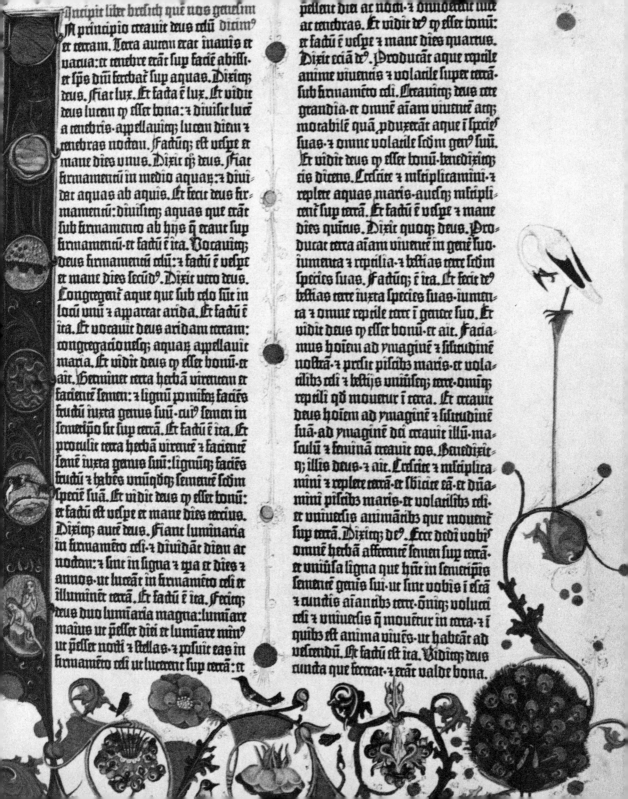

Preface

This book is a product of the author's experience in teaching the Bible at Temple University, at LeMoyne College, and at Florida International University. I have used several of the standard textbooks in teaching biblical studies, but have come to believe that there are two ways in which many of these do not serve the beginning student's needs: first, they often seem to assume a previous knowledge of the form and contents of the Bible which many of my students have not possessed; second, they have appeared to be primarily interested in matters of ancient history, culture, and literary genre which have seemed esoteric to students whose interest has not been to become scholars but to learn to read the Bible for themselves. Increasingly, I have looked for a sort of "how to" book which would not replace the standard textbooks or do what they do well, but which might precede their use as an introduction to the form and features of the English Bible, and to ways by which the Bible might be read intelligently and meaningfully by the non-specialist.

The Bible: An Owner's Manual is designed to serve a purpose like that of manuals supplied with new automobiles and appliances: to introduce the features of the new possession and to show how they may be used. Its first chapter introduces the format of the English Bible and discusses the different contents of Catholic, Protestant, and Orthodox versions. The next chapter describes the history of biblical translations and reviews several important versions which are currently available. The third chapter describes the several kinds of footnotes which are found in some Bibles and explains how they may be understood and used. The fourth chapter surveys the history of the interpretation of the

1

Bible and suggests ways that the Bible may be used today. The last chapter describes several options for continuing study and presents an annotated bibliography of resources from which the reader might select. The intention of this book is primarily practical: to show the reader how to find his way around the contents of the Bible, how to select a translation, how to deal with footnotes indicating translational or textual difficulties, how to begin to use the Bible in one's own theological or devotional reflection, and how to choose resources for further study.

Except where the contrary is indicated, biblical quotations in the present work are from the Revised Standard Version of the Bible, copyright © 1946, 1952, 1971, 1973, and are used by permission of the Division of Education and Ministry of the National Council of the Churches of Christ in the U.S.A.

I wish to acknowledge the contributions of several persons to the writing of this book, including Dr. Thomas F. McDaniel of the Eastern Baptist Theological Seminary, who read the drafts of several chapters and offered many constructive suggestions, and Barbara Dunevitz and Judie Sheffield, who typed the final version. My wife, Sharon R. Hann, not only provided an abundance of the spousely encouragement which authors traditionally acknowledge, but also read the draft intelligently and carefully and assisted in improving many unclear and poorly-chosen expressions. The contributions of each of these made this book a better one; the flaws it continues to have are of course my own responsibility.

1

Your New Bible

Finding Your Way Around in the Bible

It is customary for an owner's manual to give a brief description of the location of the features and controls of the product which it accompanies. With regard to the Bible such a description is especially necessary: not only is there a sometimes bewildering variation among the contents included in the Bible by different religious groups, there are often confusing differences between the systems of notation of biblical passages used in different translations, and between the names assigned to the biblical writings themselves. The paragraphs which follow will discuss these problems for the beginning reader; readers who are already familiar with the system of citation and nomenclature used in modern editions of the Bible may wish to skip to the next section of this chapter.

The Bible is a collection of independent writings which were brought together, in some cases, centuries after they had been written. In this regard, therefore, the Bible resembles an anthology of short stories more than a modern novel which follows a single narrative throughout its chapters. Christian Bibles are divided into two main sections: the Old Testament, a collection of Jewish writings from before the time of Jesus, and the New Testament, a collection of Christian writings, most of which were written in the first century following the life of Jesus.[1] The individual writings which make up the Old Testa-

---

1. Among Jewish writers, for whom there is no "newer" testament than their own Jewish Scriptures, the term "Old Testament" is not used. "Hebrew Bible" or "Scripture" is preferred.

ment and the New Testament are known as "books." This term is used despite the fact that some of these writings, such as the many letters that are included in the New Testament, are not "books" in our usual sense of the word. The New Testament is made up of twenty-seven books. The number of books in the Old Testament varies between Catholic, Protestant, and Orthodox Bibles.

With the exception of the Book of Psalms, which is itself a collection of hymns, most of the remaining books of the Bible were not originally divided into smaller units. In ancient times, quotations from the Bible (which were often made from memory) were identified simply by the name of the person thought to be the author or, even more simply, by the phrase "it is written" or its equivalent. An example of the former is the quotation which opens the Gospel of Mark:

> As it is written in Isaiah the prophet, "Behold, I send my messenger before thy face, who shall prepare thy way; the voice of one crying in the wilderness: Prepare the way of the Lord, make his paths straight. . . ."

The ambiguity of referring to "the quotation which opens the Gospel of Mark" illustrates the necessity of designating smaller divisions within the biblical books for the sake of reference and reading. Fourth and fifth century manuscripts of the New Testament divided the Gospels into smaller sections. These and other systems of dividing the text were used during the Middle Ages, usually to mark sections for reading in public worship. There was as yet no standardized way of designating a specific portion of biblical text.

The present system of dividing the biblical books into sections called "chapters"[2] was invented in the thirteenth century by Stephen Langton, who was the chancellor of the University of Paris. Langton's chapter divisions came to be used in the Parisian text of the Vulgate, the standard Latin Bible of scholars and theologians, and eventualy were adopted in other manuscripts of the Vulgate and of the Hebrew Old Testament. With the general adoption of Langton's chapters by Chris-

---

2. Since the book of Psalms is itself a collection of writings, its sections are called "psalms" rather than "chapters." The first psalm is therefore correctly called "Psalm 1" rather than "Psalms, chapter 1."

tian and Jewish translators and scholars, it became possible to designate portions of a biblical book by a system that would be understood by everyone. All translations of the Bible and writings by biblical scholars adhere to this common system. The reader may be sure that, say, Genesis 12 will be Genesis 12, no matter which Bible he or she is using.[3]

The chapter divisions of the Bible are large units, usually including the equivalent of several modern paragraphs. Once these chapters had been adopted, it became possible to divide the chapters into smaller units of text called "verses."[4] This enabled scholars to cite passages more conveniently and with greater precision. The system of subdivisions which has become standard for the Old Testament was adopted from the system which had been used by Jewish scholars to designate small units of text in the Hebrew Bible. The division of the New Testament into verses was done by Robert Estienne, a Parisian printer of the sixteenth century. Estienne's divisions of Langton's chapters first appeared in his 1551 edition of the Latin and Greek texts of the New Testament, and from there were incorporated into the standard Greek New Testament text of the period, called the *textus receptus*. It was through their widespread use in the Latin Vulgate and the Greek *textus receptus* that Langton's chapters and Estienne's verses have become the standard way of citing small units of biblical text.

The standard way of citing a biblical reference consists of the name of the biblical book or its abbreviation, followed by its chapter number and its verse number. Thus, Luke 2:14 denotes the familiar lines from the Christmas narrative in the Gospel of Luke, the second chapter, and the fourteenth verse of that chapter:

> Glory to God in the highest, and on earth peace among men with whom he is pleased.

The most common way to designate chapter and verse is with arabic numerals separated by a colon, as in the instance above. This is the

---

3. The exceptions to this uniformity exist in the Psalms, in which traditional Catholic Bibles differ from Jewish and Protestant translations in the numbering of most of the psalms.

4. The term "verse" was used even though the majority of the material in the Bible is not poetic in nature. The Psalms and portions of other books are in fact poetic, although the modern verse divisions do not always correspond with their poetic structure.

method of the King James Bible, the Jerusalem Bible, and most contemporary biblical scholars. A frequent alternative is to separate the numerals with a period ("Luke 2.14"), as in the Revised Standard Version and Today's English Version, or with a comma ("Luke 2, 14"), as in the New American Bible. An older method, not used in modern translations of the Bible but found in some writings by biblical scholars, is to designate the chapter with roman numerals and the verse with arabic ("Luke II:14"). Other systems of designating chapter and verse are occasionally found, but should not be confusing to the reader who recalls that the first number designates the chapter and the second the verse. Occasionally, a reference is found with only one number, such as Exodus 20. In almost all such cases, reference is made to the entire chapter. The only exception occurs when a book has only one chapter and the number therefore indicates the verse. This exception is not confusing in actual practice, since a reference to Obadiah 15, for example, will be clear when it is observed that the book is only one chapter long.

An important exception to the statement above that all Bibles share a common system of chapter divisions exists in the Book of Psalms. Since the book is a collection of originally separate psalms, the divisions between these psalms had already existed before the time of Langton. A problem for the reader is created by the fact that there are two different ways of numbering the psalms. In the Latin Vulgate version, which was followed in traditional Catholic translations of the psalms, the psalms which are numbered 9 and 10 in the Hebrew text are read as one single psalm. The same is true of the Hebrew Psalms 114 and 115. On the other hand, the Hebrew Psalms 116 and 117 are each divided in the Vulgate into two separate psalms. Jewish and Protestant translations have followed the Hebrew numbering of the psalms, with the result that, although all Catholic, Protestant, and Jewish Bibles contain a total of 150 psalms, not all translations number them in the same way. Eastern Orthodox Bibles contain an additional 151st Psalm.

The present work will follow the practice of most modern Bibles, including those translated by Catholic scholars, in numbering the psalms according to the Hebrew system. Among Catholic translations, the Hebrew numbering system is followed by The Jerusalem Bible, The New American Bible, and the Catholic Edition of the Revised Standard

Version.[5] The Confraternity of Christian Doctrine version follows the Vulgate system but indicates Hebrew numbering in parentheses. The oldest Catholic translation of the Old Testament into English, the Douay version, follows the Vulgate system and does not indicate the Hebrew numbers. Readers using the Douay version may locate the psalms in their Bibles by using the conversion chart in Table 1.[6]

The names of the books of the Bible are given in order in Table 3. There is a table of contents at the front of every Bible, and the reader will find this useful for locating the specific page on which a desired book begins. Some Bibles have a separate table of contents for the New Testament. If this does not appear in the front of a Bible, it may be found at the beginning of the New Testament, preceding the Gospels: Matthew, Mark, Luke, and John. Many of the books of the Old Testament are named for their subject matter, such as Genesis (the creation), the Books of Kings (the history of the Hebrew monarchies), and Psalms. Others are named for their central characters, such as Joshua, the Books of Samuel, and Ezra, or for their traditionally-ascribed author, such as Isaiah, Jeremiah, and Ezekiel. The first four books of the New Testament are narratives of the life of Jesus called "Gospels."[7] These bear the names of those traditionally thought to be their authors, Matthew, Mark, Luke, and John. Two books in the New Testament have descriptive titles, the Acts of the Apostles (a narrative about the deeds of Jesus' followers after his death) and Revelation (a series of visions ascribed to John).[8] The majority of the New Testament books are letters.

---

5. The Jerusalem Bible indicates the Vulgate numbers in the margin with a small letter "v," while the Catholic Edition of the Revised Standard Version places the Vulgate numbers in brackets.

6. Should the reader have any doubt about the numbering system used in his version of the psalms, this can be checked by examining Psalms 22 and 23. If the first line of Psalm 22 is the familiar "The Lord is my shepherd," the Vulgate system is followed and the conversion chart in Table 1 will be needed. If it is Psalm 23 which begins with these words, the Hebrew system is used and no conversion is necessary. (The Jerusalem Bible, which follows the Hebrew system, reads "Yahweh is my shepherd," using the original Hebrew divine name instead of the traditional English rendering "The Lord.")

7. This word is a modern form of the old English *god spell,* and is used to translate the Greek *euangelion,* "good tidings." Our words "evangel" and "evangelist" are derived from the latter term.

8. The Book of Revelation is sometimes incorrectly called "Revelations." The correct form is singular.

TABLE 1
CONVERTING HEBREW TO VULGATE PSALM NUMBERING

Most Bibles number the psalms according to the Hebrew system. This system may be converted to the Vulgate system used in the Douay version by using the following table:

HEBREW PSALM NUMBERS:	TO CONVERT TO VULGATE/DOUAY:
1–9	No change is needed.
10	Subtract 1 from the psalm number.[a]
11–114	Subtract 1 from the psalm number.
115	Subtract 2 from the psalm number.[b]
116:1–9	Subtract 2 from the psalm number.
116:10–19	Subtract 1 from the psalm number.[c]
117–146	Subtract 1 from the psalm number.
147:1–11	Subtract 1 from the psalm number.
147:12–20	No change is needed.[d]
148–150	No change is needed.

---

a. Hebrew Psalm 10 becomes in the Vulgate a second part of Psalm 9.
b. Hebrew Psalm 115 becomes in the Vulgate a second part of Psalm 113.
c. Hebrew Psalm 116:10–19 becomes in the Vulgate Psalm 115, with verse numbers beginning with 10.
d. Hebrew Psalm 147:12–20 becomes in the Vulgate Psalm 147, with verse numbers beginning with 12.

The largest number of these, ascribed to Paul, bear the names of their first readers, such as the Romans, the Galatians, and the Philippians. It was once thought that the Book of Hebrews was written by Paul; it too is named for its intended readers. The remaining letters are named for those thought to be their writers, such as those bearing the names of Peter and James.

Special care should be taken to distinguish those biblical books which include in their titles the words "first" and "second," such as First and Second Kings and First and Second Chronicles in the Old Testament, and First and Second Corinthians and First and Second Peter in the New Testament. The Old Testament pairs were originally one writing, but were divided into two sections for convenience in handling the scrolls on which they were written, in the same way as a modern book might be printed in two smaller volumes rather than as one larger tome. In the New Testament these paired writings are separate letters written to the same recipients, as in the case of the Corinthians, or ascribed to the same author, as in the case of Peter. The books which appear in pairs are distinguished by the arabic or roman numeral which precedes the name of the book. As an example, Second Kings may be cited as "2 Kings" or "II Kings." Each book of a pair bears its own chapter numbers. This is true even in those now-paired books which were originally one writing.

A potentially confusing situation exists in the New Testament: There are five New Testament books which, in their full titles, bear the name of John. These are:

The Gospel According to John
The First Letter of John
The Second Letter of John
The Third Letter of John
The Revelation to John.

The simplest of these to distinguish is Revelation. The name of John is normally not used in citing this book and in fact does not appear in some translations of the Bible. The Jerusalem Bible and The New American Bible, for instance, simply title this book "The Book of Revelation." The remaining four books may be easily distinguished by the absence or presence of the words "First," "Second," or "Third." A reference to "John," without an ordinal number, is to the Gospel of John. A reference with an ordinal number, such as "First John," is to one of the letters ascribed to John. Thus, a reader would find the reference "John 1:3" in the Gospel of John toward the beginning of the New Testament, and "1 John 1:3" in the First Letter of John toward its end.

A final matter to be considered in connection with finding one's way around in the Bible is the fact that not all translations call the biblical books by the same names. For instance, the Revised Standard Version contains two books bearing the name "Chronicles." There are no books by that name in the Douay version. The Douay Bible names the corresponding books "Paralipomenon." With one exception, these differences occur only in the Old Testament, and were caused by the fact that, in the early centuries of Christianity, the Old Testament of the Greek-speaking Christians was a Greek translation called the Septuagint. This Greek translation naturally used Greek forms in translating biblical names, just as English translations today use English equivalents like "John" in place of their original forms like "Yohanan." The two sets of names used for some books have resulted from the fact that some translations, such as the Douay in the case of Paralipomenon, have rendered the traditional Greek forms of the names into English, whereas others, such as the Revised Standard Version, have translated the name directly into English from their original form in Hebrew.

Several of the differences between names consist only of spelling variations, and should not be confusing to the reader. Examples include Josue for Joshua, Ezechiel for Ezekiel, and Habacuc for Habakkuk. Several names whose Hebrew forms ended with the letters "-iah" were given the corresponding Greek masculine endings "-ias."[9] These include Isaias for Isaiah, Jeremias for Jeremiah, and (with an additional spelling change) Abdias for Obadiah. Other variations preserve the

---

9. The Hebrew name ending "-iah" means "Yahweh" or "the Lord." The name Zechariah comes from the verb *zachar,* "remember," and means "The Lord remembers." In Greek, however, a name ending in an *a*-sound is normally feminine, so the Hebrew "-iah" ending was replaced by the Greek masculine ending "-ias." (A similar gender distinction is preserved in English in the difference between "Julia" and "Julius.")

titles given to some books by their Greek translators. For instance, the Books of Samuel and Kings, which were separate books in Hebrew, were put together by the Greek translators under a title which meant "kingdoms." Most Bibles follow the Hebrew nomenclature for these books; the Douay version, however, preserves the Greek system of considering the books as a single unit by designating the books not 1, 2 Samuel and 1, 2 Kings but 1, 2, 3, and 4 Kings. The variation between "Chronicles" and "Paralipomenon" has a similar origin: "Chronicles" translates the original Hebrew title meaning "events of the past," while "Paralipomenon" preserves the Greek title meaning "things omitted (from the narrative given in Samuel and Kings)." The single variation in the New Testament is in the name of its last book: the original title in Greek, "Apokalupsis," has been anglicized by the Douay version as "Apocalypse," while other translations have translated the Greek title by its English equivalent, "Revelation." The present work will follow the practice of Jewish, Protestant, and recent Catholic translators; readers of older Catholic translations will be assisted by the conversion chart found in Table 2.

The Contents of Your Bible

One of the facts which often strike a purchaser of the Bible is the large variety of Bibles on the market today in bindings ranging from traditional leather to contemporary denim, and bearing titles from the sedate "The Holy Bible" to the more lively "Good News for Modern Man." A less apparent but more significant variety exists with regard to the contents of the Bible. Among the several religious groups which use the Bible as their authority there is no complete consensus of opinion as to which collection of writings is to be considered the authoritative Scriptures.

The term used to designate the recognized Scriptures of a religion is "canon." This term is an English form of the Greek *kanōn,* which originally meant a reed. Since a reed could be used for taking measurements, *kanōn* came also to mean a measuring stick, a ruler, or a standard. In biblical studies, a canon is the standard list or collection of writings that make up the Bible. While a religion may also find other

TABLE 2
CONVERTING COMMON TO DOUAY
BIBLICAL NOMENCLATURE

Recent biblical translations share a common system for naming the books of the Bible. The following chart may be used to convert these names to those used in the Douay and other Catholic translations. Books whose titles differ among translations are listed alphabetically by their common names. A complete sequential listing of the biblical books is found in Table 3.

COMMON NAME:	DOUAY NAME:	ALSO USED BY:
1, 2 Chronicles	1, 2 Paralipomenon	CCD[a]
Ezekiel	Ezechiel	CCD
Ezra	1 Esdras	CCD[b]
Habakkuk	Habacuc	CCD
Haggai	Aggeus	CCD
Hosea	Osee	CCD
Isaiah	Isaias	CCD
Jeremiah	Jeremias	CCD
Jonah	Jonas	CCD
Joshua	Josue	CCD
1, 2 Kings	3, 4 Kings	CCD
1, 2 Maccabees[c]	1, 2 Machabees	CCD
Malachi	Malachias	CCD
Micah	Micheas	CCD
Nehemiah[d]	2 Esdras	—
Obadiah	Abdias	CCD
Revelation	Apocalypse	CCD
1, 2 Samuel	1, 2 Kings	—
Sirach	Ecclesiasticus	JB[e]
Song of Solomon[f]	Canticle of Canticles	CCD
Tobit[c]	Tobias	—
Zechariah	Zacharias	CCD
Zephaniah	Sophonias	CCD

a. CCD=Confraternity of Christian Doctrine Version
b. Ezra is known simply as "Esdras," without the ordinal number, in the CCD Version.
c. These books and others, called "deuterocanonical," are not found in all Bibles. See the following section of this chapter.
d. Nehemiah is known as "Nehemias" in the CCD Version.
e. JB=The Jerusalem Bible.
f. The Song of Solomon is sometimes called "The Song of Songs," as in the Jerusalem Bible and the New American Bible. The book is usually cited as "Song."

writings to be useful, only canonical writings are regarded as scriptural and as having final religious authority.

The question of which writings are canonical is not new. At least three distinct canons existed in pre-Christian Judaism. The smallest canon was that of the Samaritans. The Samaritans were a small sect which the Jews of the time of Jesus had ceased to recognize as a valid form of Judaism.[10] The Samaritan canon consisted of only the five books attributed to Moses: Genesis, Exodus, Leviticus, Numbers, and Deuteronomy. The Samaritan text of these books differed slightly from other Jewish versions, mostly in the interest of making the Samaritans appear to be the legitimate successors of the religion of Moses.

A somewhat larger canon of Scripture was held by the Pharisees, a sect which eventually became the authoritative interpreters of Judaism. The Pharisees had long accepted the five Mosaic books as authoritative, calling them the Torah or the Law.[11] In addition to these books, the Pharisees' canon included a second collection of writings which recorded the history of the Hebrew people from the death of Moses to the end of the Hebrew prophets. Since the Pharisees believed themselves to be the successors to the Old Testament prophets, it was natural that they included the prophets' teachings and the related history to be authoritative.[12]

By the end of the first century A.D., a third group of writings had begun to be recognized by the Pharisees. This collection included the

---

10. The religious animosity which existed between Samaritans and Jews was used by Jesus as the basis of his parable about the good Samaritan (Luke 10:30–37). The Samaritans still exist as a separate sect, and have been described by Shemaryahu Talmon's article, "The Samaritans," *Scientific American* 236:16 (January 1977), pp. 100–108.

11. The Hebrew word *torah* means "instruction"; the concept is that the Old Testament Law is the instruction given by a loving God to his people. The familiar Christian understanding that the law is burdensome should be balanced by reading such passages as Deuteronomy 4:7–10 and 30:12–14.

12. The Pharisees identified themselves as the inheritors of the teachings of Moses and the prophets in the following: "Moses received Torah from Sinai and handed it on to Joshua, and Joshua to the elders, and the elders to the prophets, and the prophets handed it on to the men of the Great Assembly (believed to have been the immediate ancestors of the Pharisaic movement)." This quotation is from an early collection of Pharisaic traditions called *Pirke Aboth*. A convenient English translation is Judah Goldin's *The Living Talmud: The Wisdom of the Fathers* (New York: New American Library, Mentor Books, 1957).

Psalms, a history of the Hebrews' return from exile in Babylon in 538 B.C., a history of the Hebrew monarchy written from the perspective of those returnees, and a book of visions written in the name of the prophet Daniel. After considerable discussion about several of these books (including the Song of Solomon, which some thought to be too erotic, and Esther, which does not mention God), these books were finally accepted and became the third section of the present Hebrew canon.[13]

Although the Pharisees and their successors in rabbinic and modern Judaism accepted only these three divisions as forming the canon of the Bible, the Jews of Alexandria in Egypt had a larger canon. By the third century B.C., the Alexandrian Jews had become so assimilated to their Greek-speaking culture that they were no longer able to read their Scriptures in Hebrew. It was therefore necessary to translate the Bible into Greek, which was becoming the common literary language of the Mediterranean world. Since it had been said that this Greek translation of the Old Testament had been made by seventy or seventy-two scholars, it came to be known as the Septuagint, a name derived from the Greek word for seventy.[14]

The Septuagint included several writings which were not in the canon of the Pharisees of Judea. These included books of later Hebrew history, stories about Jewish heroes, books of theology and practical philosophy, and expanded versions of Daniel and Esther. (The additions to Esther in the Septuagint soothed orthodox sensitivities by explicitly identifying God to be the cause of the narrative's events.) Several of the

---

13. Since the Hebrew names of the three parts of the canon are *Torah* (Law), *Nebi'im* (Prophets), and *Kethubim* (Writings), the Hebrew Bible is sometimes known by the acronym *Tanak.* The fact that the Writings had not yet officially become part of the canon is reflected in the common New Testament name for the Old Testament, "the Law and the Prophets." (Matthew 5:17, "Think not that I have come to abolish the law and the prophets," is the first of many such citations.)

14. The Septuagint is commonly designated in writing by "LXX," the roman numeral for seventy. The *Letter of Aristeas,* written during the second century B.C., stated that the Greek translation of the Torah was made at the request of the royal librarian by 72 scholars in 72 days. The Alexandrian Jewish philosopher Philo (around 20 B.C. to 40 A.D.) said that it was translated by divine initiative and guidance so that the translation is equal to the original Hebrew text as the inspired word of God. The Alexandrian Jews were not alone in their ignorance of Hebrew; the fact that the Septuagint was the standard Old Testament for most Jewish Christians of the first century indicates that this ignorance was widespread.

writings in the Septuagint were obviously added to the Alexandrian canon after the original translation. Second Maccabees, the Wisdom of Solomon, and the additions to Esther were originally composed in Greek, for example, and the Book of Sirach, which had been written in Hebrew, had been translated into Greek by its author's grandson. The books which are found in the Septuagint but not in the Hebrew canon are called "deuterocanonical," a term which means "belonging to the second canon."[15]

Although Judaism eventually rejected the Septuagint and the Alexandrian canon, these were preserved by a religious movement which had adopted them second-hand from their original owner: the Christian Church. Although the original Christians were Aramaic-speaking Jews from Judea,[16] the spread of Christianity among Greek-speaking Jews and non-Jews of the Mediterranean world resulted in Greek replacing Aramaic as the language of the Christian movement. Evidence of this is the fact that all of the writings of the New Testament, written during the years from 50 to 125 A.D., were composed in Greek.[17] The translation and the canon of the Greek-speaking synagogue became the Old Testament of the Greek-speaking Church. The inclusion of the deuterocanonical books within the Christian Old Testament had the weight of established usage and tradition in later Christianity. The deuterocanonical books were explicitly included in the Old Testament canon which was defined by the Roman Catholic Council of Trent in 1546.

The issue of the canon of the Old Testament was taken up again by the Protestant reformers. Since the reformers denied that the Church was an infallible guide for Christian faith, it was necessary to define where a reliable guide was to be found. The reformers' doctrine was that the Bible was the sole authority for Christians. In contrast to the

---

15. Since, as will be seen below, the deuterocanonical books are not recognized as canonical by Protestants, they are sometimes called "apocryphal," a term which means "hidden." Several of the deuterocanonical books were circulated in Judea, but without canonical status. Portions of the Greek texts of Tobit and Wisdom, and of the Hebrew text of Sirach, have been found at archaeological sites.

16. Aramaic, a semitic language related to Hebrew, had become the common spoken language among Jews in Palestine during the time of Jesus.

17. Most of the New Testament was written during the first half of this period. Second Peter may have been written as late as 150 A.D.

TABLE 3
THE CONTENTS OF THE BIBLE

I. THE OLD TESTAMENT

The Catholic version of the Old Testament differs from the Hebrew Bible by including the deuterocanonical books, and by arranging the books in a somewhat different order. The Protestant Old Testament has the same books as the Hebrew Bible, but preserves the arrangement of the Catholic version.[a]

HEBREW BIBLE	CATHOLIC OLD TESTAMENT	PROTESTANT OLD TESTAMENT
Genesis	Genesis	Genesis
Exodus	Exodus	Exodus
Leviticus	Leviticus	Leviticus
Numbers	Numbers	Numbers
Deuteronomy	Deuteronomy	Deuteronomy
Joshua	Joshua	Joshua
Judges	Judges	Judges
1, 2 Samuel	Ruth	Ruth
1, 2 Kings	1, 2 Samuel	1, 2 Samuel
Isaiah	1, 2 Kings	1, 2 Kings
Jeremiah	1, 2 Chronicles	1, 2 Chronicles
Ezekiel	Ezra	Ezra
Hosea	Nehemiah	Nehemiah
Joel	Tobit	Esther
Amos	Judith	Job
Obadiah	Esther	Psalms
Jonah	1, 2 Maccabees[b]	Proverbs
Micah	Job	Ecclesiastes
Nahum	Psalms	Song of Solomon
Habakkuk	Proverbs	Isaiah
Zephaniah	Ecclesiastes	Jeremiah
Haggai	Song of Solomon	Lamentations
Zechariah	Wisdom	Ezekiel
Malachi	Sirach	Daniel
Psalms	Isaiah	Hosea
Job	Jeremiah	Joel
Proverbs	Lamentations	Amos
Ruth	Baruch	Obadiah
Song of Solomon	Ezekiel	Jonah
Ecclesiastes	Daniel	Micah
Lamentations	Hosea	Nahum

HEBREW BIBLE	CATHOLIC OLD TESTAMENT	PROTESTANT OLD TESTAMENT
Esther	Joel	Habakkuk
Daniel	Amos	Zephaniah
Ezra	Obadiah	Haggai
Nehemiah	Jonah	Zechariah
1, 2 Chronicles	Micah	Malachi
	Nahum	
	Habakkuk	
	Zephaniah	
	Haggai	
	Zechariah	
	Malachi[b]	

II. THE NEW TESTAMENT

All versions of the New Testament include the same contents and follow the same arrangement.[c]

Matthew	1, 2 Thessalonians
Mark	1, 2 Timothy
Luke	Titus
John	Philemon
Acts	Hebrews
Romans	James
1, 2 Corinthians	1, 2 Peter
Galatians	1, 2, 3 John
Ephesians	Jude
Philippians	Revelation
Colossians	

a. Several additional books are contained in the Eastern Orthodox Bibles. These are Third Maccabees, a narrative about Jews in Egypt during the third century B.C., and Fourth Maccabees, a book of philosophy and ethics. The Hebrew Bible is composed of the sections: the Law (Genesis through Deuteronomy), the Prophets (Joshua through Malachi), and the Writings (Psalms through 1, 2 Chronicles). Christian versions of the Old Testament preserve the order of the Greek canon, and are arranged in the order: the Law (Genesis through Deuteronomy), the Historical Books (Joshua through Esther or 1, 2 Maccabees [see following note]), the Poetical and Wisdom Books (Job through Proverbs [Job through Sirach in Catholic Bibles]), and the Prophets (Isaiah through Malachi).

b. Catholic versions differ in their location of 1, 2 Maccabees. The Jerusalem Bible and the New American Bible place the books of the Maccabees following Esther, as in the table above. The Douay version, the Confraternity of Christian Doctrine translation, and the Catholic Edition of the Revised Standard Version place these books following Malachi.

c. The New Testament is arranged in the order: the Gospels (Matthew through John), a history of the early Church (Acts), the letters traditionally ascribed to Paul (identified by their recipients, Romans through Hebrews), the general or catholic letters (identified by those traditionally identified as their authors, James through Jude), and a book of prophecy (Revelation).

Catholic position that the Church was the divinely-authorized interpreter of the Bible, the Protestants insisted that the Bible needed no external interpretation. The reformers' position is reflected in the following statement from the Westminster Confession of Faith of 1646: "All things in Scripture are not alike plain in themselves . . . yet those things which are necessary to be known, believed, and observed for salvation, are so clearly propounded, and opened in some place of Scripture or other, that not only the learned, but the unlearned, in a due use of the ordinary means, may attain unto a sufficient understanding of them."

Since the reformers had denied that the Church and its tradition was infallible, it was impossible for them to accept the traditional canon without question. The argument of John Calvin is representative of the reformers' position: the Old Testament of the Christian Church is based, not on tradition, but on the practice of Jesus and the apostles; and the Bible of Jesus and the apostles was the Hebrew Bible with its shorter canon of recognized books. Calvin was pleased to note that, contrary to the unanimity which was presumed by the Council of Trent, the issue of the deuterocanonical books was never fully settled in the ancient Church. Calvin observed that St. Jerome, who had done the Latin Vulgate translation, had believed that the deuterocanonical books did not have the same canonical status as the writings of the Hebrew Bible.[18]

Many early Protestants continued to include the deuterocanonical books in their translations of the Bible but with the notation that these books did not have full canonical status. Martin Luther placed the books at the end of his German translation of the Old Testament with the statement, "These are books which are not held equal to the sacred Scriptures, and yet are useful and good for reading." English translations of the Bible by Protestants initially included the deuterocanonical

---

18. Jerome included the deuterocanonical books in his translation on the authority of the Church, and noted, "The Church reads them for the edification of the people." The reformers' appeal to the practice of Jesus and the apostles is not as conclusive as they had supposed: the deuterocanonical Book of Wisdom is quoted or used several times in the New Testament (Wisdom 5:16–18; [Ephesians 6:11–14], 9:15 [2 Corinthians 5:4], 13:1–9 and 14:22–31 [Romans 1:20–32]). This does not necessarily imply that Wisdom (and, in addition, the rest of the Greek canon) were considered canonical by the first Christians: the matter is complicated further by the fact that Jude 14–15 quotes directly from 1 Enoch, a Jewish writing which is found in no denomination's canon of Scripture.

books (usually in a separate section called "Apocrypha" at the end of the Old Testament), but during the seventeenth century these books began to be omitted completely from Protestant Bibles. Since early in the nineteenth century, Protestants have included in their Bibles only those books which the reformers believed to be canonical: the New Testament, and the books of the Old Testament according to the Hebrew canon. Table 3 lists the books of the Bible in sequence as they are found in Hebrew, Catholic, and Protestant Bibles. Throughout the present work, the term "Bible" will be used to denote the Christian canon of the Old and New Testaments, without distinction between the larger and shorter versions of the Old Testament.

Sing a new song to the Lord,
  for he has worked wonders.
· His right hand and his holy arm
  have brought salvation.

· The Lord has made known his salvation;
  has shown his justice to the nations.
· He has remembered his truth and love
  for the house of Israel.

· All the ends of the earth have seen
  the salvation of our God.
· Shout to the Lord, all the earth,
  ring out your joy.

· Sing psalms to the Lord with the harp,
  with the sound of music.
· With trumpets and the sound of the horn
  acclaim the King, the Lord.

2

Which Translation?

The reader of this book may notice an occasional note identifying the specific translation from which a quotation has been taken or adapted. As the present paragraph is being written, the table beside my desk holds five different translations of the Christian Bible. These are the King James Version (translated in 1611), the Revised Standard Version (New Testament 1945, Old Testament 1952), the Jerusalem Bible (1966), the New American Bible (1970), and Today's English Version (1976). There are other translations on my bookshelves and still others in the university library. A person who notices this variety may well feel some bewilderment and may be inclined to wonder just which Bible is to be taken to be the source of Christian faith and practice. The present chapter will assist the reader in sorting through the variety of biblical translations by surveying the history of the translation of the Bible, examining why new biblical translations are made, and describing some of the differences between biblical translations. A concluding portion of this chapter will evaluate several contemporary translations for use by the general reader.

The Early Translations

Christians have read translations of the Bible almost from the beginning of the Christian movement. The earliest translation used by Christians was the Greek translation of the Old Testament called Septuagint. This translation, which came to be the standard Old Testament of Greek-speaking Christians, had been produced by Jewish scholars during the third century before Christ. Christians themselves began to translate when the sayings of Jesus and other early Christian materials, which were originally spoken in Aramaic, were put into Greek and incorporated into the Greek writings of the New Testament. There are several instances in the New Testament where sayings are preserved in Aramaic and then translated into Greek. These occur most frequently in Mark, and include Jesus' miracle-working words *Talitha, cumi,* "Little girl, stand up," and *Ephphatha,* "Be opened," of Mark 5:41 and 7:34.[1] Other Marcan instances are *Abba,* "Father," of Mark 14:36 and Jesus' words from the cross *Elohi, Elohi, lama sabachthani?* ("My God, my God, why have you forsaken me?) of Mark 15:34.[2] Paul uses *Abba,* "Father," in Romans 8:15 and Galatians 4:6, and in 1 Corinthians 16:22 preserves without translation the Aramaic prayer *Marana tha,* "Lord, come."

The earliest translations of the Bible into a language other than Greek were made as a result of the Church's missionary activity. Although Greek was the common literary language of most of the Mediterranean world, the Christian message traveled to places where other languages were read and spoken. Among these were Edessa (now in Syria) and the surrounding areas in the Parthian Empire northeast of Judea in which the common language was Syriac, and the Roman colonies in north Africa, in which Latin was the standard tongue.

One of the earliest centers of Christianity outside of Judea was the city of Antioch in the Roman province of Syria. This city had been founded by one of the successors to Alexander the Great and was a center of Greek culture. According to Acts 11:19–26, the Christians who first came to Antioch to avoid a purge in Jerusalem actively began to convert both Jews and non-Jews of Antioch to their Christian faith. Antioch subsequently became a base for Christian missionary activity throughout the region and the eastern Mediterranean. The language of the Christian community in Antioch was Greek: it was in Antioch that the followers of Jesus were first given the Greek title *hoi Christianoi,*

---

1. The preservation of these miracle-working sayings in their original Aramaic has led some to speculate that they were used in Aramaic among Greek-speaking Christians as magical incantations. See Morton Smith, *Jesus the Magician* (San Francisco: Harper, 1978), p. 95.

2. The Aramaic saying is itself a translation into Aramaic of the Hebrew of Psalm 22:1.

"the Christians," and the letters written in the early second century by Ignatius, the bishop of Antioch, were in that language.

During the second century, Christianity began to spread eastward from Antioch into the Syrian outback and beyond. By the end of that century the Gospel had reached Edessa. Since the common language of that region was Syriac instead of Greek, it became necessary to translate the New Testament into that language. Syriac is a semitic language similar to the Aramaic spoken by Jesus and his first followers. One of the earliest translations of the New Testament into Syriac was the *Diatessaron* of Tatian, which was a harmonized compilation of the four Gospels, made toward the end of the second century. A later Syriac version of the Bible, called the *Peshitta,* has become the standard biblical text of the Syrian Church.

The first translation of the Bible into Latin was made not in Rome, but in the Roman colonies along the northern coast of Africa. The city of Carthage had been founded as a Phoenician colony during the ninth century B.C. This colony became an independent state after the decline of Phoenicia and, during the third and second centuries B.C., challenged the expanding power of Roman navies in the central Mediterranean. When Carthage finally fell to Rome in 146 B.C., its territory became the Roman province of Africa, and it was settled by Latin-speaking Roman citizens, who exploited the region's agricultural resources. Although in Rome itself educated persons learned Greek, the same was not true in Roman north Africa. Romans in Africa continued to rely on Latin, and so when Christianity advanced into that region its communication of the Gospel had to be in that language. The first Christian to write extensively in Latin was Tertullian of Carthage, who lived during the late second and early third centuries. The Bible which Tertullian used was Greek. By the middle of the third century, however, a Latin translation of the Greek Bible had been made, and was the source of the over 1,500 biblical quotations found in the writings of Cyprian, the bishop of Carthage.

The language of the Christians in Rome itself was originally Greek. Paul's letter to the Roman Christians was in Greek, as were the writings of the Christians of Rome until the middle of the third century. In Roman society those who were the most likely to know Greek were the educated members of the aristocracy, who had learned the language as part of their education, and the lower class immigrants from the east, whose Greek was the commonly spoken *Koinē* dialect rather than the refined language of the classical authors. The earliest Christians in Rome fit into the latter category; the Roman Church began as the community of Christians who had migrated to Rome and who had brought their faith with them.[3] The latinization of the Church of Rome was a gradual process which began in the first century with the conversion of native Romans and which was completed in the fourth century with the adoption of a Latin liturgy for its worship. By the second century, Christianity, which was still largely a foreigner's religion, had attracted a large number of native Latin speakers. By the third century, Latin was used for the pastoral letters of the bishops of the city. It may be that the latinization of the liturgy took place at some time after the common language of Roman Christians had already become Latin. An additional factor preventing the earlier use of a Latin service at Rome may have been the use of Latin in the pagan cults. Only after paganism had been outlawed in Rome in 355 could the language which had been used in pagan worship be adopted by the Christian Church.

Since Latin had become the language of many Christians in Rome and in the West before it became the official language of the Church, it is to be expected that the earliest Latin translations of the Bible were made unofficially and for local use. These early versions, which are now called "Old Latin," varied considerably in quality. Augustine complained that everyone who knew a little Greek and Latin, and who had access to a Greek Bible, dared to attempt a translation. It was the fact of the large number and uncertain quality of the existing Latin translations of the Bible which led Pope Damasus, who had previously established the use of Latin in the liturgy in Rome, to commission a standard, officially-sanctioned Latin Bible.

---

3. The Roman attitude was that Christians were simply a part of a larger number of undesirables from the East who had moved into their city. The writer Juvenal stated, "I cannot abide a Rome of Greeks; and yet what fraction of our dregs comes from Greece?" (Satire 3:60, quoted in John Gager, *Kingdom and Community* [Englewood Cliffs, N.J.: Prentice Hall, 1975], p. 102). This attitude contributed to the atmosphere which fed the later persecutions of the Church.

The primary translator of the new Latin Bible was Eusebius Hieronymus, who is known to us as Jerome. Jerome had studied in Rome and had later learned Hebrew at Antioch. The first portion of the Bible to be completed by Jerome was the Gospels, in which he attempted as much as possible to retain the familiar Old Latin renderings of the text. His translation of the Psalms, with which he began his work on the Old Testament, was immediately adopted for use in the liturgy in Rome. As Jerome proceeded to translate other portions of the Old Testament from the Greek Septuagint into Latin, he became convinced that the Old Testament should be translated directly from Hebrew into Latin. This decision disturbed several of his contemporaries, including Augustine, who wondered whether Jerome was implying that the Greek Old Testament, which had been used by Christians for centuries, was not fully inspired. In spite of this and other criticisms, Jerome's translation was used broadly throughout the West, and came to be known as the "Vulgate," the "common" version of the Latin Bible. In 1546 the Roman Catholic Council of Trent reaffirmed the status of the Vulgate by declaring it to be the authentic Bible of the Church.

Although portions of the Bible including the Gospels and Psalms had been translated into English earlier, the first English version of the entire Bible was produced by John Wycliffe and several of his colleagues in the Lollard movement between 1380 and 1382. This translation was made from the Vulgate and not from the original languages. Since the Lollards advocated social and religious reform, they soon encountered opposition, and Wycliffe's translation was condemned and its copies were burned. In 1525 William Tyndale completed a translation of the New Testament from Greek. This version ran afoul of the authorities and was suppressed, and its translator was put to death. The first English Bible to be officially sanctioned was that of Miles Coverdale, which was based on the work of Tyndale. Coverdale's first edition, published in 1535, was dedicated to King Henry VIII; the next edition, in 1537, was published with the king's license.

From the translation of Wycliffe's Bible in 1380 until the publication of Coverdale's translation about a hundred and fifty years later, the history of English translations of the Bible was one of suppression. This suppression occurred under both Catholic and Anglican auspices (Henry VIII initially feared that an English Bible would be too Lutheran), and the modern reader may wonder why this was so. There were in principle no compelling reasons why Bibles in the vernacular had to be forbidden. Portions of the Bible had been translated much earlier into Old English, and Bibles were openly printed in other European languages including German, Dutch, French, Italian, and Portuguese. The only other country in Western Europe in which vernacular Bibles were suppressed as a matter of policy was Spain under the Inquisition. The instances of Spain and of England between 1380 and 1535 must therefore be seen as exceptions rather than as the normal policy.

One reason for the suppression of vernacular Bibles had to do with the Church's understanding of the role of the Bible in the Church. The Bible was considered to be the source document of the Christian faith and God's revelation to the Church, but it was not thought that this message needed to be read privately by each individual Christian. The message of the Bible was to be taught to the people by the Church, which was thought to have been given this responsibility and authority by Christ. The experience of the Church had been that individuals who attempted to interpret the Bible apart from the Church's guidance tended to misunderstand parts of the Scripture or to become involved in heresy, and so many thought it wiser to restrict direct access to the Bible to those who were trained to interpret it correctly.[4]

There may have been a related reason for the suppression of English Bibles during the fourteenth and fifteenth centuries. Since the invasion of England by the Normans in the eleventh century, English had virtually ceased to be a literary language. The Norman aristocracy spoke French, and they considered English to be the barbaric tongue of the people they had conquered. Those who were literate read French

---

4. The English Catholics and the early Anglicans both feared that the Bible would be misunderstood by the uneducated. It was later recognized by both Protestants and Catholics that the danger of private Bible reading was not as severe as it had been thought in the fourteenth and fifteenth centuries, and private reading came to be encouraged by both communions. This realization, however, had not taken place before the early 1500's, and it is unfair to judge churchmen of that age by the standards and insights of our own.

and Latin, so the production of literature in English was for a long time thought to be unnecessary.[5] In the social climate of the late fourteenth century, moreover, an English translation of the Bible may have seemed not only to be novel but revolutionary. Wycliffe's translation appeared at the time of a peasants' revolt, during which the archbishop of Canterbury and other high officials were killed. Although Wycliffe himself did not support this rebellion, his criticism of the economic injustices of the time, together with his translation of the Bible into the language of the rebels, must have led many to conclude that a Bible in the people's language was not only religiously but also politically dangerous. Once an English Bible became associated with potential sedition as well as potential heresy, the suppression of subsequent translations would be assured.[6]

The most influential English Bibles were the Catholic Douay Version, which began to be printed in 1582, and the Protestant King James Version of 1611. Significantly, both translations appeared as responses to the sectarian use of previous English translations of the Bible. The century following the Protestant Reformation was not a time of moderation in religious matters, and translators, like others, were inclined to take sides. Since the Protestant Geneva Bible of 1557 had identified the "angel of the bottomless pit" of Revelation 9:11 as the Pope, it was almost to be expected that the Catholic Douay translators would respond in kind by appending to Jesus' saying in Matthew 6:24, "No one can serve two masters," the marginal comment, "Two religions, God and Baal, Christ and Calvin, The Catholic Church and Heretical Conventicles." It was a breakthrough that served objectivity when the royal mandate to the King James translators of 1611 included the rule that no marginal notes were to be added except "for the explanation of the

---

5. Wycliffe's translation was a milestone in English literature as well as in biblical translation. Its novelty may perhaps be appreciated by noting that it preceded by several years the writing of Chaucer's *Canterbury Tales.*

6. It is most interesting to speculate that if Wycliffe had rendered the Bible into Norman French instead of into English, it might have occasioned no disturbance at all. The fears of the traditional religionists and royalists would have seemed to have been confirmed when the Puritan army of Oliver Cromwell, English translations of the Bible in hand, deposed and then executed King Charles I in 1649.

Hebrew or Greek which cannot without some circumlocution, so briefly and fitly be express'd in the text."

The primary factor motivating the exiled Catholic scholars at the English College at Douai in Flanders to produce an English translation of the Bible was the unacceptability to Catholics of existing translations. Not only did previous versions like the Geneva Bible include anti-Catholic notes, these Bibles were often the work of a few unauthorized individuals, and of uncertain quality and reliability. The college began its work on the New Testament while it was temporarily located at Rheims, and the New Testament was published there in 1582. The Old Testament was published in 1609 and 1610 after the college had returned to Douai.[7] The Douay Bible was translated from the Latin Vulgate and not from the original languages. Catholic scholars insisted, with justification, that the standard Latin text of the Vulgate was a more reliable basis for a translation than the printed Greek texts of uncertain ancestry which were beginning to circulate among scholars.[8]

One of the purposes of the Douay translators was to provide an English translation for use in Catholic preaching and religious instruction. Accordingly, the translators frequently used technical Catholic theological terms to render the Latin of the Vulgate into English. The use of these terms was intended to reflect not only the meaning of the biblical words but also the way they were understood in the continuing tradition of Catholic theology. An example may be found in Matthew 3:1–2. The Revised Standard Version of these verses reads: "In those days came John the Baptist, preaching in the wilderness of Judea, 'Repent, for the kingdom of heaven is at hand.'" The Greek term rendered "repent" is *metanoeite,* and denotes a change in the direction of one's life. John is here saying, in a manner reminiscent of that of the

7. Technically, this Bible consists of the Rheims Old Testament and the Douay New Testament; together these are known as the Douay-Rheims Bible. The names of the places where these were first published were originally printed as "Douay" for Douai and "Rhemes" for Rheims. The spelling of the former and the pronunciation of both were retained, to the effect that the common way of pronouncing the version's full name sounds like "Douay Reams."

8. The first published edition of the Greek New Testament was that of Erasmus in 1516. This text was hastily prepared and contained hundreds of typographical and other errors. This text, however, was widely circulated, and was for many years the standard Greek text of the New Testament.

Old Testament prophets, that one's life is to be transformed in obedience to God. The Douay Bible reads "do penance" in place of "repent." This term implies the Catholic sacrament of reconciliation, in which a person confesses his sins to a priest and performs an assigned duty as a means of amending his life. To the critics, the introduction of this sacramental term into the text has appeared to be an inappropriate anachronism, reflecting the perspective of later theology and not the sense of the original text.[9]

The translators of the Douay Bible were careful to state that their reasons for offering their translation were not the same as those of the Protestants, who believed that a vernacular Bible was essential to the well-being of the Church. In fact, commenting on the religious turmoil that had been brought about by the Reformation, they observed that it might have been better if the Bible had remained in Latin. Since, however, English translations had begun to be made, it was their concern that English-speaking Catholics have access to a version which would be useful to them and not subversive to their faith. The Douay Bible was subsequently revised on several occasions and, with these revisions, remained until recent time the standard Bible of English-speaking Catholics.

The most influential Bible in English was the King James Version of 1611. Shortly after King James VI of Scotland became monarch of the United Kingdom as James I of England in 1604, he convened a conference of Protestant leaders to discuss the condition of the Church of England. Among the suggestions which the meeting produced was that of providing a new version of the English Bible, since the existing translations were considered to be "corrupt and not answerable to the truth of the original." On February 10, 1604, James ordered that the new translation be made, and a group of scholars was named to begin the work. The Church of England in the time of James was embroiled in theological controversy between Puritans and high churchmen, and representatives from both sides were appointed to be among the transla-

---

9. The Douay translators were following the Vulgate which reads *poenitentiam agite.* Among modern Catholic translations, the New American Bible reads "Reform your lives," while the Jerusalem Bible reads "Repent," with a footnote stating that the term "implies a change of heart."

tors. The new Bible was to be translated directly from the Hebrew and the Greek, and its language was to follow as closely as possible the familiar usage of earlier English Bibles, especially that of the Bishops' Bible of 1568.

The translators of the King James Bible worked carefully. Six committees were assigned different portions of the Bible. Each portion was initially translated by each scholar working separately. Their initial drafts were discussed by the full committee which in turn produced a final draft representing the committee's consensus. Cross-references were included in the new Bible but, as has been noted above, there were no marginal notes except for those needed to clarify the meaning of the words of the original texts. The translators followed the literary style of the original texts closely. This was done in the interest of accuracy, and allows the reader to observe some of the grammatical features of the original text. Particularly in the New Testament, however, the resulting renderings often string together long series of clauses in a manner which is normal in Greek but sometimes confusing to the beginning English reader. In spite of this and other weaknesses of the King James Bible, this version has become a landmark both of English literature and of biblical translation. The carefulness and objectivity of its translators enabled it to be used as the standard English Bible for Protestants of all denominations until the publication of the Revised Standard Version in the mid-twentieth century.

Why Are There New Translations?

The fact that the Douay and King James Bibles became the standard biblical translations for English-speaking Catholics and Protestants, respectively, raises the following question: If the translators of these versions did their work competently and carefully, and if their efforts have been so broadly recognized by later Christians, why is it that newer translations of the Bible continue to be produced? Indeed, one may be inclined to conclude that the effort spent in producing seemingly redundant new Bibles could well be directed elsewhere in other areas of concern.

There are at least three major reasons why newer translations continue to be necessary. The first of these is that we are in a better situation by far than were the translators of these classic versions with regard to our knowledge of the original text of the Scriptures. The King James translators took pains to produce an accurate translation, even to the extent of italicizing words which seemed to be necessary in English but which were not in the original languages. In spite of the translators' best efforts, however, the Greek text from which they worked contained many errors, and was not a reliable representative of the words of the original biblical authors. The King James translators, for example, cannot be faulted for translating Romans 8:1 as: "There *is* therefore now no condemnation to them which are in Christ Jesus, who walk not after the flesh, but after the spirit." This translation is a precise rendering of the Greek text which they were translating, and even notes that the verb "is," which is required in English but not in Greek, was not in their text. The problem with this translation is that the words, "who walk not after the flesh, but after the spirit," are not found in the best Greek manuscripts of this passage. The Greek texts which were available to scholars in the sixteenth and seventeenth centuries were generally of a poor quality. We now have far better manuscripts available to us, and can correct deficiencies in the King James Version which were produced by errors in its texts. The technique of studying manuscripts in order to recover the most accurate reading is called "textual criticism" and will be discussed in the next chapter of this book.

As we have seen, the poor quality of the available Greek texts was, as has been noted, one of the reasons why the Douay Bible was translated from the Latin Vulgate, which had been preserved with care by the Church. The tools of textual criticism have also been used in Catholic biblical scholarship. On the one hand, the text of the Vulgate itself has been subjected to textual examination, and we are now in a better position than were the Douay translators to know what the Latin Bible produced by Jerome and his colleagues actually said. In addition, recent Catholic versions, including the Jerusalem Bible and the New American Bible, have come to be translated directly from Hebrew and Greek. The practice of recent Catholic scholars has been to regard the original biblical languages as the basic sources for biblical translation, and to consider the Latin Vulgate to represent an ancient stage in Catholic theological reflection on the text. Among both Catholics and Protestants, advances in our knowledge of the biblical text have enabled scholars to produce translations which more accurately render into English what the biblical writers actually intended to communicate.

A second reason why new translations continue to be necessary is our improved knowledge of the language and vocabulary which the biblical writers used. It was long recognized that the Greek of the New Testament was written in a dialect different from that of the classical Greek authors, but as recently as the end of the nineteenth century, no one knew what this dialect represented. Some thought that New Testament Greek was a kind of semitic Greek which was influenced by the Aramaic-speaking backgrounds of its writers. Others suggested that it was a special form of Greek which had been created by God for the revealing of his word. (One writer called it "Holy Spirit Greek.") Toward the end of the nineteenth century, however, archaeologists began to discover large numbers of Greek letters, commercial documents, and other writings which were written in the same dialect as the New Testament. The initial result of these discoveries was that it became possible to identify what the Greek of the New Testament was. Far from being a special religious dialect, it was the common everyday form of Greek writing during the time when the New Testament was written. This dialect was the Greek which had been spread throughout the Mediterranean by the conquests of Alexander the Great, and which on the one hand had been somewhat simplified grammatically and enriched lexically by the influence of its new cosmopolitan environment. Since this dialect was the common Greek of the first and later centuries, it is called "Koinē," from the Greek term *koinē,* "common."

The most important result of the discovery of these ancient Koinē writings was that it became possible to get a clearer understanding of what the words of the New Testament originally meant. Although there are a few words in the New Testament which seem to have been coined by the early Christians themselves, its writers in the vast majority of cases used the common language of their readers. Since scholars can now see how these words were generally used in the Hellenistic culture in which the New Testament was written, they can arrive at a more precise understanding of how they were intended to be understood by the writers of the New Testament.

A third reason why new translations continue to be made is that the English language itself has continued to change, and that the words used by the older translators no longer convey the meanings which the translators intended. An annoying inconvenience for modern readers is the presence in the Douay and King James Bibles of archaic pronouns and verbs, the frequent use of "thee," "thou," and "-eth" that seems to us to be characteristic of biblical or religious language.[10] These, however, while perhaps troublesome, are not likely to mislead the reader. What can be even more confusing, however, is the fact that some of the words used in the older translations no longer mean to us what they meant to the translators, and so we may read them and think that we have understood, when in fact we have misunderstood what the ancient writer and the older translator wanted to say.

An example of the confusion that may result from changed English usage is the King James Version of 2 Thessalonians 2:7: "For the mystery of iniquity doth already work: only he who now *letteth will let,* until he be taken out of the way." The modern reader would be justified in concluding that the writer is talking about a being who permits sin to occur, and who will someday be taken away. The Greek behind the italicized words, however, does not mean "he who permits," but "he who restrains." The reference is not to one who permits evil but to the spirit, who restrains it. The Revised Standard Version renders the meaning intended by the King James translators more adequately for the modern reader: "he who restrains it will do so until he is out of the way."[11] In this instance, the modern reader of the King James Bible would have

---

10. The older English versions were actually more precise and preserved some of the grammatical precision of the original languages. "Thou" and "thee" are singular, and "ye" and "you" are plural. "Thou" and "ye" are nominative, used for the subjects of sentences. "Thee" and "you" are objective, used for the objects. The "thou shalts" of the Ten Commandments are singular, addressed to each individual Hebrew. Modern English blurs this precision, using "you" for all these functions.

11. This particular problem does not exist for the reader of the Douay Bible, which renders the participle "he who now holdeth."

concluded just the opposite of what its author and its translators intended to communicate.

Advances in our knowledge of the original text of the Bible and its language, as well as changes in our own English idiom, continue to make new translations necessary. But what sort of translations will these new versions be? Several preliminary considerations will determine what kind of a Bible the translator will produce. The first of these concerns the text from which he or she will be working. As we will see in the following chapter, there are no standard Greek and Hebrew texts from which all translators work. The closest to these which exist are several critical Hebrew and Greek editions, in which scholars have attempted to reconstruct the original wording from the evidence of the presently-existing manuscripts and other ancient citations. Translators must decide whether to base their work on the judgments of the editors of one of these critical texts, as was done in the case of Today's English Version, or to make their own informed selections from among the various readings of the manuscripts, as did the translators of the New American Bible. Some translations explicitly identify the texts from which they were made; even when this is not the case, however, decisions about the text must be made before the work of translation itself can begin.

A more practical factor that will affect the nature of a proposed translation is its intended readership. It is an unfortunate fact that not everyone who has received a high school diploma can read well, although others can read very well indeed. In addition, even among the most literate members of the population there are some who are unfamiliar with some of the more specialized vocabulary of the Christian faith. Most translators in the past seem to have presumed that their readers would have experienced no difficulty in working through long and sometimes difficult English renderings of biblical sentences. The King James Version, for instance, sometimes uses expressions which reproduce the construction of the original languages but which are unusual or difficult in English. One example is the unfortunate expression, "I am a man who am a Jew," found in Acts 21:39. In addition, some versions have rendered the technical vocabulary of the original languages by equally difficult English terms. An example may be observed in 1 John 2:2, where it is stated that Jesus Christ is the *hilasmos* for our sins. This Greek word is taken from the sacrificial ritual, and is translated "propitiation" by the King James and Douay-Rheims versions and "expiation" by the Revised Standard Version, terms hardly more intelligible than *hilasmos* for the non-specialized reader. The meaning of *hilasmos* is rendered into English without complication by "an offering for our sins" (New American Bible), "the sacrifice that takes our sins away" (Jerusalem Bible), "the means by which our sins are forgiven" (Today's English Version), and "the remedy for the defilement of our sins" (New English Bible).[12] Features such as these often make the older translations difficult for the non-specialized and not-well-educated reader to understand.

A third factor which will determine the sort of translation which is produced is the translator's conception of what a translation is. At first thought, the matter seems obvious: a translation is what is produced when something originally written in one language is put into English. The question becomes more complex when it is asked just what it is that the translator intends to render into English. Is it the words of the original author or is it the concept of the author for which his words are only the vehicles of expression? If the translator believes that his task is to render the words of the original author into English, he is most likely to attempt a word-for-word or "formal equivalence" translation.[13] Such a translation aims at adhering as closely as possible to the form of the original writing and may go so far as to reproduce expressions or grammatical forms which are found in the original but which are unusual or difficult in English. The Revised Standard, Douay, and King James Versions are examples of verbal equivalence translations. (The difficult features of the King James Version which we observed in the preceding paragraph are the result of the translators' efforts to repro-

---

12. See the articles, "Propitiation" and "Expiation" in the *Interpreter's Dictionary of the Bible,* and the discussion by Eugene A. Nida in his *Good News for Everyone* (Waco, Texas: Word Books, 1977), p. 73.

13. A formal equivalence translation is sometimes popularly called "literal." This term is misleading for two reasons: first, the term "literal" is best reserved for a method of biblical interpretation to be discussed in Chapter 4, to avoid confusion; and, second, because it implies that the alternatives to such a translation are "non-literal" or haphazard.

duce the structure of the original texts.) Implicit in a decision to produce a word-for-word translation may be the assumption that the translator's reader will be a well-educated and religiously well-grounded person who will be able to follow the English parallels to the complex sentences often found in Greek, and who will require little assistance with technical terms and allusions which might have been clear to the passage's first readers.

Many contemporary scholars have come to recognize that translating is a more complex matter than the finding of an English term which means the same as a word in the Hebrew or Greek original, and seek instead to render the author's concepts into language in which it would naturally have been expressed in English, even when this may require different forms and expressions from what the original-language author himself used. This approach to translating is called "dynamic equivalence" and employs contemporary structural linguistic theory. In this view, there is no such thing as the "true" meaning of a word. Words are socially agreed-upon symbols for communication and have no meanings apart from the intention of their users.[14] A translator who is seeking a dynamic equivalence will seek to identify all the facets of meaning intended by the original author and to render these as they would naturally be expressed in English.

In his introductory handbook to Today's English Version, Eugene Nida considers the example of Mark 1:4.[15] In the Revised Standard Version, this verse reads: "John the baptizer appeared in the wilderness, preaching a baptism of repentance for the forgiveness of sins." What did the author of this sentence intend to say? As Nida analyzes the units of meaning found in the verse, he finds the following:

John preaches (that which follows)
John baptizes the people

---

14. This point was made by the German philosopher Ludwig Wittgenstein, who observed that, in most cases, the meaning of a word is its use in the language. A word means what its users intend to communicate, and is not governed by any abstraction beyond that.

15. Nida, *Good News,* pp. 97–104.

The people repent
God forgives the people
The people sin

Today's English Version seeks to express these concepts the way they would naturally be written in English: "So John appeared in the desert, baptizing and preaching. 'Turn away from your sins and be baptized,' he told the people, 'and God will forgive your sins.'" The dynamic-equivalence translator will ask, "Has anything been omitted from what the author intended to say? Has anything been added?" If the answer to both of these is "no," then it will be argued that a faithful translation has been made. Although the principles underlying the translation of modern Bibles have seldom been spelled out as fully as Nida has done in the case of Today's English Version, similar approaches to translating have informed the translators of the Jerusalem Bible and the New English Bible.[16]

Reviewing Translations of the Bible

In the remaining section of the present chapter, attention will be given to nine classical and contemporary translations of the Bible: the King James Version of 1611, the Confraternity of Christian Doctrine revision of the Douay-Rheims Version, published in 1941, the Revised Standard Version of 1952 (NT 1945), the Jerusalem Bible of 1966, the New American Bible and New English Bible of 1970, the Living Bible paraphrase of 1971 (NT 1962), Today's English Version of 1976 (NT, *Good News for Modern Man,* 1966), and the New International Version of 1978 (NT 1973). General observations will be made about each of these translations, including an examination of how each renders the complex Greek of the first two verses of the Letter to the Hebrews.

The King James Version. The origins and characteristics of this version have been discussed above, and the comments made there need

---

16. Lamar Williamson, Jr., "Translations and Interpretation: New Testament," *Interpretation* 37:2 (1978), 163–164.

not be repeated. An example of the translators' work may be seen in Hebrews 1:1–2:

> God, who at sundry times and in divers manners spake in time past unto the fathers by the prophets, Hath in these last days spoken unto us by *his* Son, whom he hath appointed heir of all things, by whom also he made the worlds;

The Greek of this passage consists of a complex set of clauses, participles, and finite verbs. The subject, "God," appears in verse 1; the main verb, "spoke," does not occur until verse 2, twelve words later. The care taken by the translators to reproduce the original as closely as possible in English may be seen in this quotation: the italicized "his" indicates that the word had to be added to conform to English usage, and the translators wanted the reader to know that it was not in the Greek. In addition, the translators adhered closely to the order of the Greek words, producing a sentence as long and complex as the original (note the final semicolon: the sentence will continue for two more verses). The Greek reader of this passage was assisted by inflectional forms which exist in that language but not in modern English; the reader of the King James Version must sort his way through the sentence without such helps. Finally, we may observe the version's use of now-archaic words and endings. Words such as "divers" and forms such as "hath" are no longer commonly used in English and, although perhaps not unintelligible, present a barrier to the reader who is not familiar with seventeenth-century usage. For these reasons, the King James Version is, in spite of its long-term popularity, not the most useful version of the Bible for the general reader. Ironically, it is this version which, until recently, was given to elementary-school children in Protestant Sunday Schools.

The Confraternity of Christian Doctrine Version. The Douay-Rheims Bible, the classical Catholic translation into English, was revised by Bishop Richard Challoner in 1750. The resulting version, known as the "Challoner-Rheims" version, was authorized for use by American Catholics in 1810. As early as 1829, however, it was recognized that changes in the English language made it desirable that further revisions be made. Its final revision, published in 1941 as the

Confraternity of Christian Doctrine Version, is the last of the English-language versions to be based on the Latin Vulgate.

The Confraternity of Christian Doctrine Version translates Hebrews 1:1–2 in the following way:

> God, who at sundry times and in divers manners spoke in times past to the fathers by the prophets, last of all in these days has spoken to us by his Son, whom he appointed heir of all things, by whom also he made the world;

The English translators of the King James Version often followed the renderings of the Douay-Rheims Bible, upon which the Confraternity Version was based, and the relationship between these translations may be observed in comparing their versions of this passage. The most obvious differences consist in the modernization of the verb endings. (The archaic "divers," however, is retained.) Another change in the interest of understanding is the Confraternity Version's division of the material into paragraphs of meaning, instead of arbitrarily into verses. The most important differences may be seen in the Latin-based phrase "last of all in these days" in place of the King James reading "in these last days." The footnote explains that the reading of the text follows the Latin, and the Greek reading is provided.

In terms of modern English usage, the Confraternity Version represents an improvement over both the Douay-Rheims, its parent version, and the King James Version. (Among its changes is that "repent" is read in place of the Douay-Rheims' "do penance" at Matthew 3:2.) The greatest weakness of this version is that it is a revision of a translation from the Latin instead of a translation from the original biblical languages. Although the Latin text may have been argued in the seventeenth century to have been at least as reliable as the Greek and Hebrew manuscripts then available, the same could not be said today. When a papal encyclical in 1943 allowed Catholic biblical translators to work directly from the original languages, the Confraternity Version was rendered obsolete shortly after its publication. While copies of this translation still exist in Catholic circles, it has nothing except historical interest to recommend it over the more recent Catholic translations to be discussed below.

The Revised Standard Version. The King James Version of 1611 was revised on several occasions. Some of the revisions were made responsibly by groups of scholars; others were done less responsibly by individuals, sometimes to express a particular doctrinal interest. Among the great revisions of the King James Version were the English Revised Version of 1881–85 and the American Standard Version of 1901. The English revisers were determined to preserve the style of the 1611 translation, while taking account of changes in the English language and of advances in textual scholarship. The American members of the committee which had produced the English Revised Version continued to work after its completion, and published their further revised version in 1901. This version, which was noted for its precision, was conspicuous in reading "Jehovah" where the older translations had read the more familiar "Lord."[17] Great advances in biblical scholarship took place in the first part of the twentieth century, and in 1937 the International Council of Religious Education, the holders of the copyright of the American Standard Version, authorized a revision of the Bible which would become known as the Revised Standard Version. The New Testament was published in 1945, followed by the Old Testament in 1952. The text of the Revised Standard Version has been altered further in more recent editions, in part on the basis of advances in textual scholarship. An important ecumenical step in 1973 was the publication of an RSV "Common Bible," which included the deuterocanonical books found in Catholic Bibles but traditionally omitted by Protestants. An expanded edition of the RSV in 1977 contained the additional books recognized by the Eastern Orthodox churches. For the first time since the Reformation, a Bible has become available for all English-speaking Christians, and has received the commendation of leaders of all major branches of Christianity. The RSV has become widely used, and is the

---

17. The name of God in biblical Hebrew is *Yahweh.* The consonants of this word eventually came to be combined with the vowels of another word, *adonai,* which meant "Lord." The resulting form, when spelled in a Latin manner, came to be written "Jehovah." "Jehovah" was never used as a name for God in the Old Testament.

translation most often cited in writings by contemporary biblical scholars.

The extent to which the Revised Standard Version has improved upon the King James Version may be observed in its rendering of Hebrews 1:1–2.

> In many and various ways God spoke of old to our fathers by the prophets; but in these last days he has spoken to us by a Son, whom he appointed the heir of all things, through whom also he created the world.

The archaic "sundry" and "divers" are gone, together with the obsolete verb endings. The long Greek participial phrase which the King James translators rendered "who at sundry times and divers manners spake in time past unto the fathers by the prophets" has become a coordinate clause in a more manageable compound sentence. The sentence which in Greek continues for two more verses has been divided, as indicated by the terminal punctuation ending the quotation above.[18] The "his," which has been supplied by the 1611 translators in the absence of a Greek article or possessive pronoun, has been replaced by the more accurate "a." The Revised Standard Version follows the practice of other modern translations of dividing its text by paragraphs instead of by verses. The translators sought to provide a formal equivalence translation within the limits imposed by the difference between the Greek and English languages. Its correspondence to the structure of the original languages has made the RSV a useful translation for persons engaged in detailed grammatical and exegetical studies of the text.

The Jerusalem Bible. The Jerusalem Bible is the first Roman Catholic English translation to have been made directly from the original biblical languages instead of from the Latin of the Vulgate. Its publication in English was stimulated by the great popularity of the French-

---

18. These changes do not make the RSV a less accurate translation than the KJV: the Greek "many-ways and various-ways formerly God having-spoken to the fathers by the prophets...." is simply not acceptable English, and must be recast in some way by any translator.

language *La Bible de Jérusalem,* which had been published in 1956 by Dominican scholars of *l'École Biblique* in Jerusalem. The Jerusalem Bible has an unusual linguistic heritage: the English text itself was translated from the biblical languages, employing the text and the translation principles used by the French translators, whereas the copious introductory materials and notes were translated from the original French version, and have in places been updated.

The Jerusalem Bible's translation of Hebrews 1:1–2 reads:

> At various times in the past and in various different ways, God spoke to our ancestors through the prophets; but • in our own time, the last days, he has spoken to us through his Son, the Son that he has appointed to inherit everything and through whom he made everything that is.[19]

The freshness and independence of this version is apparent in this quotation. The translators have not restricted themselves to the structure of the original Greek: "the Son" is repeated to become the subject of the final clause, and "our own time, the last days" renders the Greek words which the Revised Standard Version more closely represents by "these last days." A peculiar feature of the Old Testament of the Jerusalem Bible is its retention of the Hebrew name *Yahweh* for God instead of reading "Lord" in accordance with more familiar English usage.[20] A few scholarly reviewers have criticized some of the translators' decisions in textual matters. An example may be observed in John 2:12, in which the Greek texts state that Jesus went to Capernaum "with his mother and [his] brothers and his disciples" (the second "his" is not found in all manuscripts). A traditional Catholic doctrine is that Mary was perpetually a virgin: that she remained celibate and childless even after the birth of Jesus. Accordingly, Catholic commentators have usu-

---

19. The raised dot preceding "in" marks the beginning of the next verse; the numbers themselves are in the margin.

20. Around the time of Jesus Jews began to avoid pronouncing "Yahweh" to avoid even the accidental misuse of the name (Exodus 20:7). The Greek translation of the Old Testament used by the early Christians read "Lord" in place of the divine name, and so it became customary for Christians to use "Lord" even when *Yahweh*" appeared in the Hebrew text itself.

ally understood Jesus' "brothers" to be his stepbrothers or cousins, or his disciples, none of which does damage to the range of meanings which the Greek word can have. In John 2:12, however, it is unlikely that "brothers" means "disciples," since the latter are also mentioned in the same sentence. The Jerusalem Bible's reading, "with his mother and the brothers," allows the reader to assume that "the brothers" are not Jesus' siblings but his followers. This reading has no support in the Greek manuscripts, and it is difficult to avoid the conclusion that it was adopted in the interest of traditional Catholic theology.[21] The Jerusalem Bible was translated by Catholic scholars for a Catholic readership. Catholics will find it and its often denominationally-oriented notes useful; Protestants may be expected to find it less so.

The New American Bible. In 1943 the papal encyclical *Divino Afflante Spiritu* allowed Catholic biblical translators to work directly from the original languages. Accordingly, a group of Catholic scholars, eight of whom had been members of the team which had produced the Confraternity of Christian Doctrine version just three years earlier, began in 1944 to translate the New American Bible. Following the decree of the Second Vatican Council that "translations be produced in cooperation with separated brethren," four Protestant scholars later became part of the translation team. Early portions of the translation began to appear in 1950; the whole Bible (with some of its earlier-translated portions having been revised) was published in 1970. The New American Bible is in every way a new translation, not dependent on an earlier version either in English or (as is the Jerusalem Bible) in another modern language.

The following is Hebrews 1:1–2 according to the New American Bible:

In time past, God spoke in fragmentary and varied ways to our fathers through the prophets; in this, the final age, he has spoken to us through his Son, whom he has made heir of all things and through whom he first created the universe.

---

21. So Robert G. Bratcher, "One Bible in Many Translations," *Interpretation* 32:7 (1978), 118.

Like the Jerusalem Bible, the New American Bible seeks clarity in English expression instead of conformity to the idiom of the original language: the Greek which the Revised Standard Version renders as "in these last days" is translated "in this, the final age." In addition, the translators' interpretative judgment may be seen in "in fragmentary and varied ways." Since the author of the passage is contrasting what he believes to be the inferiority of the Mosaic revelation to the superiority of the revelation in Christ, the translators have made a particular aspect of the contrast explicit in "fragmentary." The Greek word itself, as may be inferred from the variety of renderings which we have observed, is ambiguous. It is clear that the author of Hebrews believes the old revelation to be incomplete or fragmentary (8:1–7); it is the opinion of the translators that this view, explicit elsewhere in Hebrews, is implied in 1:1 as well, and they have made this explicit in their translation of the verse.

The New American Bible has made use of recent studies in the biblical text, and often provides useful explanatory notes. An example of the latter is the note at John 1:19, which points out that "the Jews" who are Jesus' opponents are not the whole Jewish people as such, and that the Gospel's use of the term reflects the polemic situation between Christians and Jews at the end of the first century. A few notes, such as the comment on Jesus' brothers and sisters at Mark 6:1–6, are of Catholic theological interest, but these will not be troublesome to non-Catholics.

The New English Bible. In 1946 the General Assembly of the Church of Scotland (the parent denomination of the Presbyterian churches in North America) adopted a recommendation that a new translation of the Bible "be made in the language of the present day." By the following year, representatives from the Church of Scotland, the Methodist, Baptist, and Congregational Churches, and the Church of England (the parent denomination of the Episcopal Church) had created a Joint Committee on a New Translation. The New English Bible was from its inception intended to be a new translation, and not a revision of an earlier version. The translators were aware that not all of their readers would be specialists in Christian vocabulary and declared in the Introduction to their New Testament that their version was intended for readers "whether familiar with the Bible or not."

The New English Bible translates Hebrews 1:1–2 as:

When in former times God spoke to our forefathers, he spoke in fragmentary and varied fashion through the prophets. But in this the final age he has spoken to us in the Son whom he has made heir to the whole universe, and through whom he created all orders of existence:

The translators of the New English Bible intended to produce a dynamic-equivalence version, but candidly recognized the difficulties in all such projects: "We have found that in practice this frequently compelled us to make decisions where the older method of translation allowed a comfortable ambiguity. In such places we have been aware that we have taken a risk, but we have thought it our duty to take the risk rather than remain on the fence." Examples of interpretative decisions made by the translators include "fragmentary ... fashion," "the whole universe," and "all orders of existence." The first of these is similar to the New American Bible's rendering, which was discussed above. The second and last represent the translators' views of how the author would have put in English what was originally expressed by the Greek words which meant "all things" and "the world." One may or may not agree with these renderings, but it is characteristically necessary to make such interpretative judgments in the producing of dynamic-equivalence translations. Some technical objections have been raised against the New English Bible's textual and interpretative decisions,[22] but this translation has in general been favorably received. Its popularity is reflected by the report that an entire British printing of a million copies was sold out in a single day.

The Living Bible. The Living Bible, which became such a commercial success that it was featured in the *Wall Street Journal,* is not a translation at all. Its popularity, however, has been such as to warrant inclusion in this review of biblical translations. The Living Bible is the

---

22. See, for instance, Robert G. Bratcher, "One Bible in Many Translations," pp. 199–221; K. R. Crim, "Versions, English," *IDB* Suppl., 934. One reviewer is reported to have commented that the reader wanting to know what the Bible means might consult the New English Bible; but the reader wanting to know what it says should look elsewhere.

product of a single individual, Kenneth Taylor, who has attempted "to say as exactly as possible what the writers of the Scriptures meant, and to say it simply, expanding where necessary for a clear understanding by the modern reader." The theological perspective underlying the Living Bible is what its author calls "a rigid evangelical position."

The character of the Living Bible can be observed by an examination of its handling of Hebrews 1:1–2:

> Long ago God spoke in many different ways to our fathers through the prophets [in visions, dreams, and even face to face], telling them little about his plans. But now in these days he has spoken to us through his Son to whom he has given everything, and through whom he made the world and everything there is.

The footnote to the bracketed words reads, "Implied." Portions of this rendering are suggestive of what one might expect of a dynamic-equivalence translation: "Long ago God spoke in many different ways," "his Son to whom he has given everything," "the world and everything there is." The Living Bible, however, is not a translation from the original languages at all, but a paraphrase based on the King James Version. Its author states that he wants to say "as exactly as possible" what the biblical writers intended to communicate, but, without access to the original languages, he brings us no closer to them than the 1611 translation which he used. Furthermore, Taylor demonstrates, in spite of his claim that he has consulted biblical scholars, that he has not really done his homework. His claim at John 13:23 that "all commentators" agree with his view of the authorship of that Gospel is simply incorrect. In addition, a serious charge, made both by scholars who share Taylor's theological views as well as by those who do not, is that his principle of "expanding where necessary" imports into the text ideas that simply do not exist in the original writings.[23] In addition to the words bracketed in Hebrews 1:1–2, one may observe "telling them little by little about his plans." (That God's revelation in the Old Testament was partial is

---

23. "A Dozen Bibles," *Christianity Today* 23:2 (1978) 21.

implied in the text; that it was a progressive unfolding is not.) Another instance of textual alternation is the Living Bible's introduction of a reference to the Old and New Testaments into Matthew 13:52.

Any of the dynamic-equivalence translations reviewed in this section will assist the reader in the way that Taylor intended the Living Bible to do; none will mislead the reader in the way the Living Bible occasionally will. There can be no reason to dissent from Robert Bratcher's conclusions: "Not even a paraphraser has the right to import into the text what is not clearly there, and he has even less right to import what is clearly not there—and this Taylor has done too often."[24] The Living Bible, for all its success as a publishing venture, offers no contribution to the reader interested in exploring what the writers of the Bible themselves meant and said.

Today's English Version. The New Testament of Today's English Version was translated by Robert Bratcher of the American Bible Society in consultation with a number of other scholars, and was published in 1966 under the title, *Good News for Modern Man.* This New Testament was originally sold for the at-cost price of twenty-five cents a copy! The Old Testament was translated by a team of scholars headed by Bratcher, at the request of the United Bible Societies, and was published in 1976. An edition issued in 1979 which included the deuterocanonical books has received the official approval of the bishop of Hartford, Connecticut for use by Roman Catholics. As has been observed above, Today's English Version was from its beginning intended to be a dynamic-equivalence translation. Its translators, who were chosen for their professional experience as biblical translators, were attentive to matters of language. Care was taken to produce renderings that sounded well when read aloud and which would be easily intelligible even to persons unfamiliar with traditional "biblical" language.

Today's English Version of Hebrews 1:1–2 reads:

> In the past God spoke to our ancestors many times and in many
> ways through the prophets, but in these last days he has spoken
> to us through his Son. He is the one through whom God created

---

24. Bratcher, "One Bible," pp. 125–126.

the universe, the one whom God has chosen to possess all things at the end.

It will be recalled that a goal of dynamic equivalence is to express the writer's intended meaning as he would have written it in modern English. Today's English Version exhibits the greatest independence from the sentence structure of the original languages of any translation reviewed thus far. It will be recalled that the criterion for the accuracy and faithfulness of a dynamic-equivalence translation is whether everything has been expressed of the author's intended meaning, and not whether the original-language structure has been preserved in English. The present instance demonstrates that, using this standard, Today's English Version can be recognized to be an accurate translation of the message of the biblical author. This translation has made good use of recent textual scholarship, and, while its reviewers have recognized the distinctive strengths and weaknesses of a dynamic-equivalence translation, it has generally been received well. Its care to employ common English idiom has made Today's English Version a particularly good choice for the less-experienced Bible reader.

The New International Version. Ironically, one of the problems facing some modern biblical translations has been created by the very advances in scholarship which made the new versions necessary. Advances in our knowledge of the text and language of the Bible have led translators to change some traditional readings which had seemed to some to be basic to the Christian faith. Instances of new readings which some found disturbing are the substitution of "expiation" for "propitiation" in the Revised Standard Version of 1 John 2:2 and the places in Today's English Version where the Greek word *haima* was translated by some term other than "blood." In each of these cases, some critics thought that the traditional doctrines about Christ's atoning sacrifice had been compromised, and suggestions came to be made that the newer translations had been corrupted by the views of theological liberals among their translators. In 1965, a group of conservative Protestants initiated a project, which came to be sponsored by the New York International Bible Society, to make a new translation of the Bible by scholars committed to traditional Christian doctrines as expressed in the classical Protestant creeds. The New International Version is the product of this effort.

The New International Version translates Hebrews 1:1–2 in the following way:

> In the past God spoke to our forefathers through the prophets at many times and in various ways, but in these last days he has spoken to us by his Son, whom he appointed heir of all things, and through whom he also made the universe.

The reader may be struck by the contrast between this rendering and those of the more recent translations examined above. Whereas most modern versions have in some way divided this passage into smaller and simpler sentences, the New International Version follows the form of the Greek original closely, preserving much of its structure. The translators have clearly sought to produce a formal-equivalence version like the Revised Standard Version instead of a dynamic-equivalence translation like Today's English Version. The similarity of the principles underlying this translation to those of the Revised Standard Version is reflected in the facetious remark of one conservative reviewer who, when asked why the New International Version was made, replied, "So evangelicals won't have to use the RSV."[25] Although some scholarly demurrers have been made concerning such matters as the translators' seeming retrojection of New Testament ideas back into the Old Testament, the New International Version has in general been made carefully, and may be, as one of the translators of Today's English Version has stated, "the finest fruit of American conservative scholarship."[26] The New International Version, however, is in general not an improvement over the Revised Standard Version, with which it shares formal-equivalence principles of translation. Although conservative fears that other modern translations have been theologically biased are without foundation, the New International Version may appeal to those Protestants who will be comforted by its translators' theological creden-

---

25. William LaSor, "What Kind of Version Is the New International?" *Christianity Today,* 23:2 (1978), p. 18.

26. Roger Bullard, quoted in Bratcher, "One Bible," p. 128.

tials. Other readers will not find it significantly more useful than other translations reviewed above.

Which Bible should I read? Having reviewed a number of biblical translations, if I were to be exiled to a desert island with only one version of the Bible with me, which one should it be? With three exceptions, none of those reviewed above could be considered to be a bad choice. The exceptions are the King James Version, because of its archaic and sometimes confusing English usage and its having been translated from inferior texts than those available today; the Confraternity of Christian Doctrine Version, because it was not translated from the original biblical languages; and the Living Bible, because it is not a translation at all, but a paraphrase whose author's own theological views are frequently projected upon the biblical text. The remaining translations, the Revised Standard Version, the Jerusalem Bible, the New American Bible, and New English Bible, Today's English Version, and the New International Version, are all reliable and may be useful to a Bible reader in different ways.

At this point it may be helpful to recall some of the characteristics found in Bibles translated according to formal-equivalence principles and those employing dynamic-equivalence translation theory. A Bible made according to formal-equivalence principles may preserve stylistic features which are unusual in ordinary English and which may be less easily understood, especially by the less-experienced reader; on the other hand, its translators are not as often forced to make interpretative judgments of a sort which obscure the possibility of alternative understandings of a given passage. A dynamic-equivalence Bible will usually seem more natural to the reader, and will often allow him to grasp concepts that might be obscured by classical technical expressions; but because it seeks to write the way the author would have expressed himself in English, it will be of little use to a reader attempting to do a detailed lexical or grammatical study of the original text itself. It should be clear that there is no such thing as a "right" sort of biblical translation. A translation is a tool for accessing the writer's thought. Like the jeweler's screwdriver and the hammer in my toolbox, different tools are for different tasks, and the tool selected should suit the task at hand. I use the jeweler's screwdriver to adjust my glasses and the hammer to drive picture hangers into the wall: all sorts of trouble would result from trying to use one of these for the purpose of the other!

Perhaps then we should ask: What is the purpose for which I am selecting a translation? If my purpose is to get a general overview of the thought of the author, to understand his central points and how they relate to one another, a dynamic-equivalence translation is perhaps the best choice. Such a translation is usually written in a style that will facilitate understanding, especially for the beginning reader of a portion of the Bible, and its way of handling occasionally ambiguous interpretative details will prevent these from distracting the reader's large-scale investigation of the writer's thought. But suppose instead that I were interested in examining a particular biblical passage in detail, perhaps with the aid of a dictionary or some other resource such as those described in Chapter 5 below: in such a case I would be more concerned with the words the author actually used than in what he might have written today, and a formal-equivalence translation would be the appropriate tool to select.

Among the factors to be considered in evaluating translations is the element of bias. I do not mean by this that biblical translators have intentionally skewed their work to support their own theological views. This has seldom occurred among recent biblical scholars, and it is a tribute to the objectivity of modern researchers and translators that one may read their works without becoming aware of their authors' denominational and theological affiliations. A different sort of bias, however, can exist when a translator who is accustomed to understanding the meaning of a passage in a particular way may not have seriously considered the alternative interpretations which may also exist. This danger is greater when a translation has been produced by a single scholar. It is lessened somewhat when several translators even of the same denominational or theological background collaborate, since the idiosyncrasy of any one is likely to be checked by his colleagues. The greatest objectivity is to be expected when the work of translating has involved a number of scholars of different denominations and theological views. Under such circumstances any proposal which reflects the view of a particular group rather than the meaning of the text itself is sure to be corrected by the other translators. It is therefore a step in the direction of objectivity when new Bibles have been prepared for a broad rather than a narrowly denominational readership, and have gained the approval of scholars and spokesmen of a number of religious groups. Among the formal-equivalence translations considered above only the Revised Standard Version, especially in its "Common Bible" format, approaches this standard; among the dynamic-equivalence Bibles it is most closely met by the New English Bible and Today's English Version. Any of these three, therefore, would be especially good selections for the reader of the Bible; the best choice would perhaps be the Revised Standard Version and one of the other two.

But what if I *were* to be sent to that desert island, and could take only *one* version with me: which Bible would it be? Here subjective preferences and my own study interests influence my choice. If I could have only one Bible for my own use, it would be the Revised Standard Version, probably in the format with introductory materials and notes developed by an interdenominational committee of scholars and published under the title, *The New Oxford Annotated Bible.* A better choice of a study Bible for beginning readers or for those seeking the distinctive contributions of a dynamic-equivalence translation would be the *Oxford Study Edition* of the New English Bible. These are my own preferences; those purchasing instead one of the other Bibles reviewed in this section (other than the King James, Confraternity, and Living Bible versions) will not have gone wrong.

3

Footnotes, and Such

Readers of the Bible may from time to time become curious about the marginal references or footnotes found alongside or below the text of most Bibles. Except for unadorned editions of the King James Version, which traditionally has been printed without notes, most Bibles which the reader is likely to consult have at least occasional notes or helps provided on their pages. Notes are included in Bibles for several purposes. A common sort of note offers theological or other commentary on a passage, or provides an explanation of some possibly confusing reference in the text. A second type of note is a cross-reference which cites other places in the Bible which in some way touch on the subject at hand. Still another kind of note points out alternative translations or interpretations of a word or phrase in the original language, other than that chosen by the biblical translators. Finally, a fourth sort of note concerns the original-language text itself and indicates different readings of the passage among the biblical manuscripts themselves. The first three of these different kinds of notes will require only short explanations and will be discussed in the first part of this chapter. Matters concerning the original text of the Bible are more complex and will form the subject of the chapter's final portion.

An initial observation that should be made is that notes or marginal references found in one's Bible are later additions to the text and are not part of the original writing itself. A very early set of notes which were added to the text of the Bible was the system devised by Hebrew scholars in the centuries after Jesus to indicate the pronunciation of the Hebrew of the Old Testament. Hebrew was written with consonants only, so that the familiar word *shalom* would have been spelled *slm* (the sound of "sh" and "s" were represented by the same letter). Since the latter could have been understood in many ways, including the reading "shalom" and the place name "Salem," it became necessary to indicate the correct pronunciation. This was done by a group of scholars known as the Masoretes, who added a set of dots and other marks above, below, and between the letters so that their pronunciation could be made clear without tampering with the spelling of the sacred text itself. For a long time the Masoretic vowel signs were regarded as having the same authority as the text itself. Some early Protestant scholars thought that they had been inspired by God, and they are still considered authoritative by traditional Jews. More recently, however, biblical scholars have found that, although the Masoretic vocalization is frequently correct, in some cases readings which are more likely to be original may be obtained by pronouncing the consonantal text differently. However one may understand the authority of the Bible, such authority should be understood to adhere only to the writings of the authors themselves, and not to notes or other materials which were later provided to supplement the text.

Comments, Cross-references, and Alternative Translations

Footnotes Offering Commentary. A common sort of note appended to a biblical passage offers theological commentary or is intended to shed light on some point in the passage which might be confusing. As early as the Middle Ages it had become customary to provide manuscripts of the Bible with sets of comments called *glosses.* These were usually written in the margins, but were sometimes placed between the lines, written in a different sort of letters from those found in the text itself. These annotated copies of the Scriptures were used as educational materials in the medieval schools, and by the twelfth century had become standardized. The comments found in the glosses were often of a theological nature, but could also range to other subjects such as grammar and rhetoric. The Bible was the essential textbook of the entire medieval curriculum, and the glosses' notes were used to apply the biblical text to the educational task at hand.

The early English translations of the Bible continued the tradition of providing theological commentary. As we observed in the preceding chapter, these comments came during the time of the Reformation to have decidedly sectarian overtones. The great Geneva Bible of 1560 was, as F. F. Bruce has observed, a veritable textbook of Calvinistic theology.[1] In a parallel way, the notes found in the Douay-Rheims Bible were a compendium of Catholic theology, designed to teach the doctrines of the Council of Trent to English readers who, because of Protestant persecution, were often without the guidance of Catholic pastors. The practice of Roman Catholic translators has generally preserved the medieval custom of providing notes along with the biblical text. When, in the early nineteenth century, a group of English Catholics proposed to publish an edition of the New Testament from the Douay-Rheims Bible without its usual notes and comments, they were rebuked by their bishop, who stated that the notes were a vital part of the translation, and were essential for the Bible to be "safe and profitable in the hands of the laity."[2] Catholic concerns that non-annotated Bibles were dangerous to the faith have been eased in subsequent years, and, as we have seen in the preceding chapter, editions of the Revised Standard Version without doctrinal notes have received the approval of Catholic authorities. Similar approval has been granted to the New English Bible and to Today's English Version. Catholic doctrinal notes are still available in the Jerusalem Bible and the New American Bible, which were prepared by Catholic scholars for a largely Catholic readership. (The New American Bible, as we have seen, included some Protestants among its translators.) The notes in these Bibles, though of denominational interest, are well-written and non-polemical.

It was an important step away from sectarianism in the seventeenth century when the translators of the King James Version were ordered, apparently by the king himself, to confine their marginal notes to the explanation of obscure matters of the biblical vocabulary. It was in part its omission of doctrinal commentary which allowed this Bible to be-

---

1. F. F. Bruce, *History of the Bible in English* (New York: Oxford University Press, 1978), p. 90.
2. Geddes MacGregor, *A Literary History of the Bible* (Nashville: Abingdon, 1968), pp. 250–251.

come the generally-accepted version of English-speaking Protestants of varying denominations and theological views. Protestant theology had traditionally held that the Bible was sufficiently clear in its essential teachings so as to require no external explanation, and so it became Protestant practice, following the example of the King James Version, to employ translations of the Bible with no notes of a theological nature at all.

An exception to the usual Protestant custom which was to have a great influence among American Protestants was the publication in 1917 of C. I. Scofield's *Scofield Reference Bible.* This edition of the King James Version included explanations of biblical terms, an elaborate system of cross-references, and explanations of what Scofield believed to be the most important biblical doctrines. Among the doctrines Scofield elaborated was dispensationalism, a theological interpretation of biblical history which stresses the differences, rather than the continuity, between the Old and New Testaments. This view, which was developed by the British sectarian theologian J. N. Darby, never persuaded the majority of Protestant theologians. The great popularity of the *Scofield Bible,* however, made dispensationalism a widely-believed doctrine among many conservative American Protestants, so much so that other evangelicals have complained that its acceptance has become in some circles a test of theological orthodoxy.[3] The *Scofield Reference Bible* remains popular among those who share its views; a revised edition was published in 1961. Either should be purchased only by those who are committed to dispensationalism and who choose to avoid the mainstream of contemporary biblical scholarship.

An important development in recent biblical study has been the commitment of scholars to an objective approach to the Bible, uninfluenced by one's own denominational or theological commitments. It has been this commitment which has allowed Protestants and Catholics to cooperate in the making of biblical translations. Another result of this

---

3. See E. J. Carnell, *The Case for Orthodox Theology* (Philadelphia: Westminster, 1959), pp. 117–119; Ronald H. Nash, *The New Evangelicalism* (Grand Rapids, Michigan: Zondervan, 1963), pp. 167–168. For the history of dispensationalism, see C. Norman Kraus, *Dispensationalism in America: Its Rise and Development* (Richmond: John Knox Press, 1958).

development is the possibility of collaboration in the writing of objective notes for the aid of the reader of the Bible. The character of this development may be illustrated by noting that in 1611 it was a step toward unity to omit denominationally-oriented notes from the King James Bible; we are now at a stage of understanding and objectivity where it is possible to cooperate in the making of notes without fear that they will serve sectarian denominational interests. A monument to the new objective and scholarly spirit was the *Oxford Study Edition* of the New English Bible, published in 1976. This edition combined the biblical text of the New English Bible, which had been translated in England under interdenominational auspices, with a set of notes, cross-references, and special articles by a group of American scholars. The general editor of the project was the Jewish biblical scholar Samuel Sandmel; a Protestant and a Catholic were the editors of the New Testament and the deuterocanonical books, respectively. The editors' objectives are described in their Preface: "The introductions and annotations, dealing with the literary, historical, theological, geographical, and archaeological aspects of the text, and the cross-references from one passage to another, provide the reader with ready information that should heighten his appreciation and understanding of the Scriptures.... Special articles by competent scholars in the field of biblical knowledge yield further data to enhance the reading and study of the Bible." A similar study Bible, edited by Protestant scholars but having received Catholic approval, is the *New Oxford Annotated Bible,* based on the Revised Standard Version.

How may the reader make use of the resources available in notes like these? In general, the comments made in the preceding chapter about biblical translations are also relevant here: greater objectivity is to be expected when notes represent the consensus of a number of scholars rather than the opinion of a single editor; the likelihood of objectivity is further enhanced when the editors are of several denominations instead of only one. Where these conditions do not prevail—and especially when the notes present the view of only a single commentator or viewpoint—the reader is advised to check those opinions elsewhere before accepting them as "what everyone agrees." These comments should not, however, be taken to imply that there is no value in a set of comments that represent a particular position with which the reader is in agreement. As we have noted, recent Roman Catholic Bibles frequently offer notes which represent the viewpoint of that Church. It is not inappropriate for the reader who wishes to observe or to be guided by a Roman Catholic perspective to employ such a translation in his or her study of the Bible. Such a reader should be aware, however, that the comments, like the New American Bible's treatment of the doctrine of the perpetual virginity of Mary at Luke 1:25, may represent the views of the Roman Catholic Church and not be shared by scholars of other denominations. With these observations in mind, the notes found in most modern versions of the Bible will be useful to shed light on the historical, linguistic, and cultural background of the Bible, and will therefore allow the reader to understand more clearly the message which the biblical writers intended to communicate.

Cross-References. A second sort of note found in some Bibles is a cross-reference to other places in the Scriptures where the same subject is discussed or which, in the editor's opinion, shed light on the subject at hand. An early system of cross-references was invented in the fourth century, and continued to be used through the Middle Ages. Eusebius of Caesarea divided the four Gospels of the New Testament into numbered sections and devised tables for locating passages parallel to each section in the other three Gospels. Eusebius' system, while evidently useful, was made obsolete by the introduction of chapter and verse divisions in the thirteenth and sixteenth centuries. When these divisions were generally adopted, it became possible to cite parallel passages in the margins of the biblical text without requiring the tables invented by Eusebius. Most modern biblical translations provide cross-references. These are most often found in footnotes appended to the passage to which they refer, but can occasionally be found elsewhere, such as in Today's English Version, which prints references to Gospel parallels in its paragraph headings.

The way cross-references may be used can be seen in connection with Matthew 22:41–45. This passage reads:

41 Now while the Pharisees were gathered together, Jesus asked them a question, 42 saying, "What do you think of the Christ?

Whose son is he?" They said to him, "The son of David." 43 He
said to them, "How is it then that David, inspired by the Spirit,
calls him Lord, saying,

44 'The Lord said to my Lord,
Sit at my right hand,
till I put thy enemies under thy feet'?
45 If David thus calls him Lord, how is he his son?"

There are two different kinds of cross-references which might be
sought by the reader of this passage. On the one hand, he or she might
want to know the source of the words quoted by Jesus in verse 44,
perhaps in order to study them in their original setting. On the other
hand, the reader might be interested to know which other Gospels also
report the incident reported in Matthew 22:41–45, perhaps to compare
how the dialogue is recounted elsewhere. Most Bibles will provide these
kinds of information. In the Revised Standard Version, for instance, a
note appended to verse 44 directs the reader to Psalm 110:1, the source of
Jesus' quotation, and a note to the entire passage cites Mark 12:35–37
and Luke 20:41–44 as the parallel passages in the other Synoptic Gospels
(the incident is not reported in John). A thorough set of cross-references
will, moreover, provide even more information than this. In addition to
the passages which have already been noted, the Revised Standard
Version refers the reader to Acts 2:34 and Hebrews 1:13, in which Psalm
110:1 is also quoted and applied to Jesus, and to Hebrews 10:13, a
probable allusion to the same psalm. Therefore, by consulting the cross-
references carefully, the reader will not only know where the quotation
came from and how the events are described in other Gospels, but will
also have observed those other New Testament passages where Psalm
110:1 has been applied to Jesus by their Christian authors.

It should be observed that not all Bibles offer equally thorough sets
of cross-references. The notes in Today's English Version cite only
Psalm 110:1 and the parallels to Matthew 22:41–45 in Mark and Luke,
and do not refer the reader to the other citations of Psalm 110:1 in the
New Testament. The New American Bible notes the uses of Psalm 110:1
in Acts and in Hebrews 1:13, but gives only Mark 12:35–37 as a Gospel
parallel. (A note to the latter passage, however, will direct the diligent

reader to the parallel in Luke.) An unusually thorough set of cross-references is provided in the 1959 Reference Edition of the Revised Standard Version. Its references include not only the passages discussed above, but also John 7:42, a reference to the Old Testament's prophecy that the Messiah would be a descendant of David; 2 Samuel 23:2, in which David is said to have received the spirit of the Lord (see Matthew 22:43); and 1 Corinthians 15:25 and Revelation 3:21, additional probable allusions to Psalm 110:1. It should be noted, however, that the cross-references in this edition of the Revised Standard Version are compressed into a center column between the blocks of biblical text. Although these notes are thorough, deciphering them requires a great deal of careful concentration.

In addition to parallels such as those observed above among the Gospels, parallel passages of historical interest may often be found elsewhere in the Bible. The series of books consisting of 1 and 2 Samuel and 1 and 2 Kings records the history of the Hebrews from before the monarchy to the fall of the kingdom of Judah in 586 B.C. This narrative was compiled during the Babylonian exile, perhaps by members of a Hebrew pro-reform party. A second account of much of the same history, probably written by a group of priests after the exile had ended, may be found in 1 and 2 Chronicles. Since these two histories cover many of the same events, cross-references between them should be consulted by those interested in studying the history of the Old Testament. A third set of parallels is sometimes found between the Book of Acts and the autobiographical sections of Paul's letters. Paul's conversion, for instance, is mentioned several times, including in Acts 9:1–9, 22:6–11, and 26:12–18, and in Galatians 1:11–17 and in 1 Corinthians 15:8. It is not always easy to identify which portions of Acts correspond to autobiographical references in Paul's letters, however, and caution is advised. Even though, for instance, the Revised Standard Version's cross-references to Galatians 2:1 refer the reader to Acts 15:2, it is not certain whether the visit to Jerusalem in Acts 15 is what Paul meant to describe in Galatians 2. The reader will be wise to consult a secondary resource, such as one of those described in Chapter 5 below.

Special caution should be observed in the theological use of cross-references. It will be recalled that among the passages cited in connection with Matthew 22:41–45 were Psalm 110:1, the source of Jesus' quotation, and Hebrews 1:13. Although the same words may be found in one form or another in all three passages, it should not be assumed that their authors intended them all in the same way. In Psalm 110 the words which are quoted in Matthew are part of a patriotic hymn affirming that God will defend the Hebrew king and defeat his enemies. Long after the monarchy had ended, royal psalms such as Psalm 110 came to be applied to the coming messianic king. It was in the latter sense that Jesus posed the riddle of Matthew: "How can the Messiah be the son of David and David's Lord at the same time?" Since Psalm 110 had already come to be understood messianically, the author of Hebrews can apply it to Jesus, understanding the reference to sitting on the Lord's right hand as an allusion to Jesus' resurrection. Even though Christians came to apply Psalm 110 to Jesus by using the then-common "If this is true in the lesser case (of a mortal monarch), it is even more true in the greater case (of the Lord's Messiah)" way of thinking, we should not conclude that the author of the psalm was himself thinking messianically, or that some sort of prophecy was involved. The same turn of phrase does not always mean the same thing throughout the Bible, and the presence of cross-references should not encourage the reader to infer that genuine correspondence of thought always exists among the passages cited.

Alternative Translations. A third sort of note which is frequently found in modern versions of the Bible alerts the reader to ways of rendering the text which differ from those actually chosen by the translators. An example may be observed in the first two verses of the Bible. Today's English Version of Genesis 1:1–2 reads:[4]

> In the beginning, when God created the universe,[a] the earth was formless and desolate. The raging ocean that covered everything was engulfed in total darkness, and the power of God[b] was moving over the water.

---

4. This version indicates the largest number of possible alternatives in Genesis 1:1–2. The Revised Standard Version gives only one alternative at each of the places indicated.

The notes appended to these verses read:

> [a]In the beginning ... the universe; *or* In the beginning God cre-
> ated the universe; *or* when God began to create the universe.
> [b]the power of God; *or* the spirit of God; *or* a wind from God; *or* an
> awesome wind.

The reader may well be perplexed by this variety of alternatives. If five different ways of reading the Hebrew are presented in two sentences, how can we be sure the translator knows what he is talking about?

Sometimes the reason for the seeming uncertainty of the translators is that the biblical writer himself has used an obscure term or expression, and modern scholars are unsure of what the author meant. An instance which generated some controversy is the Greek word *theopneustos* which appears in the Bible only at 2 Timothy 3:16. The King James Version had rendered the phrase in which the word is found as "All scripture *is given by inspiration of God,* and is profitable...." An alternative which appeared in the Revised Standard Version read "Every scripture *inspired by God is* also profitable." The latter seemed to some to imply that not all Scripture was inspired, and troubled those who feared that liberal theology might have influenced the new version. The problem which created the controversy was that, since *theopneustos* appears nowhere else in the Bible, it is difficult to be sure just what the author was trying to say.[5] A similar problem exists with regard to the musical direction *selah* which appears throughout the Psalms. It seems to be some sort of instruction about how the passage was originally to be performed, but no one knows exactly what it means. The practice of translators is to print *selah* untranslated or to omit the term altogether.

More frequently, the reason for the variety of possible English renderings is that the expression used by the original author includes a range of meanings for which English would use a number of different

---

5. A nineteenth-century controversy concerned whether the verbal force of *theopneustos* was to be read as passive or active: is the Scripture *inspired* or *inspiring*? See Jack B. Rogers and Donald K. McKim, *The Authority and Interpretation of the Bible* (San Francisco: Harper and Row, 1979), pp. 339–340.

terms. The translator is therefore forced to be more specific than the writer had intended to be, and must select from the whole range of possible renderings the one which he believes the author would have used if he had been writing in English.[6] The second set of alternative translations presented for Genesis 1:1–2 illustrates this difficulty. The Hebrew words used by the author are *ruach elohim.* The first of these has a range of meanings including "breath," "wind," and "spirit." The second term, *elohim,* usually means "God," but the same form can also mean "powerful" or "mighty."[7] The translator is forced by the rules governing English to make a choice among these possibilities. This choice appears in his text, and important alternatives are presented in the note. (In the case above, the translators of Today's English Version have preserved some of the enigma about *ruach* by using the general term "the power of God.")

A similar sort of difficulty frequently exists in translating Hebrew syntax. A writer using English must select a past, a present, or a future tense each time he writes a verb; this is required by the syntax of our language. Hebrew verbs, however, do not have tenses in a way which corresponds to English. Instead of expressing the relative time of an action, Hebrew verbs typically indicate whether it is complete or incomplete. One form is used for completed action, and usually (but not always) corresponds to our past tense. Another form expresses incomplete action, and is used to indicate action in the present (which is not yet complete), in the future (which has not yet even begun), or in a continuing narrative about the past (of which the outcome, from the narrator's perspective, is incomplete).[8] A further complication, which has occurred in Genesis 1:1–2, is that the form which usually corresponds to our past tense is sometimes spelled the same as an infinitive used as a verbal noun to name the act itself. Thus, the opening words of

---

6. The difficulty of selecting the correct meaning from among several is illustrated by the report that a computer which was programmed to translate from English to Russian made "The spirit is willing but the flesh is weak" come out "The wine is acceptable but the meat has gone bad."

7. In addition to these, *elohim* can also mean "gods" (of polytheistic religions), "rulers," and "judges."

8. It is not that Hebrew is incapable of precision about time: when necessary, time can be clearly indicated, usually by the addition of other words.

Genesis may be read with the verb, as "In the beginning [God] created," or with the infinitive, as "In the beginning of creating" (with the sense of "When God began to create").[9] The translator is forced by the rules of English to make choices where the Hebrew author was not explicit. In the case of Genesis 1:1–2, the translators of Today's English Version have attempted to preserve the ambiguity of the original, while alerting the reader to the alternatives by the note.

How should the reader deal with footnotes displaying alternative ways of translating a passage? Probably the least appropriate response is to select one of the alternatives on the basis of its familiarity, its compatibility with a favorite doctrinal idea, or because it "sounds right." The science of philology is a discipline requiring extensive study to master, and it is unlikely that the non-specialized reader will be able to make a reliable judgment in cases where trained scholars have had to remain uncertain. Where translational ambiguities exist, it is better to recall that central Christian teachings seldom rest upon only one biblical passage, and to resist basing one's own theological or ethical conclusions on a particular rendering where other alternatives also exist. Attempts to identify the Holy Spirit of Christian theology with the "spirit" of Genesis 1:1, for instance, are ill-advised, since we cannot be sure that the writer did not simply mean "wind." It is best to establish one's own doctrinal and ethical thought on passages where we can be better assured that we have understood what the biblical writers intended to communicate.

Textual Variations Among the Manuscripts

A puzzling feature found in some Bibles is the occasional presence of a footnote beginning with "other ancient authorities read," and continuing with a word or phrase which it seems may be substituted for the

---

9. The word for "God" follows these opening words in the Hebrew text. The verb used in past-time contexts and the infinitive discussed above are pronounced differently, and are distinguished in the Masoretic text by its vowel signs. When written without these signs, however, as Hebrew was originally written, they are often identical, as is the case in Genesis 1:1. Therefore, although we know how the word was understood by the Jewish scholars who added the vowel signs to the text, we cannot be sure how the original text itself was intended to be read.

reading of the text. These footnotes, which are most often found in the New Testament, are puzzling not only because they imply that we may not know what the author wrote, but also because the reader is unsure what to do with the information the note offers. For example, although most translations of the Bible begin the Gospel of Mark with the words, "The beginning of the Gospel of Jesus Christ, the Son of God," we are told in the Revised Standard Version that some "other ancient authorities" omit the last four words, and read simply, "The beginning of the Gospel of Jesus Christ." The question which may occur to the reader is, "If Mark began his Gospel by calling Jesus the Son of God, how could some other ancient authorities (whoever they might be) dare to leave it out?" (A more suspicious reader might wonder at the motivations of ancient scribes or modern editors, as though the status of Jesus as God's Son was somehow at stake.)[10]

The problem posed by this example is that of determining what the writer of a passage actually said in those places where the ancient manuscripts and other records of the text (the "ancient authorities" of the footnote) do not agree among themselves. The careful study of the biblical text in order to reconstruct its original wording is an important branch of biblical scholarship called "textual criticism." The word "criticism" is used to denote not a negative but an exacting attitude toward the question of the text. (It should be remembered that a literary or theater critic is one who is knowledgeable in his observations. A critic is not forbidden to reach completely positive conclusions about a particular production; what makes a critic is not that he or she is negative but that he or she is knowledgeable.)

The Problem of the Text. One way of introducing textual criticism is to ask, "How do you obtain a copy of the Bible?" Our answer is simple: we go to a bookstore and buy one. A Bible on sale in a bookstore is a printed book, produced under the same careful controls which govern the printing of other books. Type has been carefully set, galley and page proofs have been scrutinized for errors, and individual volumes are

---

10. The issue in question at Mark 1:1 is not whether Mark believed that Jesus was the Son of God. That point is made clearly in Mark's account of Jesus' baptism, in which a heavenly voice says, "Thou art my beloved Son; with thee I am well pleased" (Mark 1:11).

carefully assembled from signatures of printed pages. Except for the occurrence of an undetected typographical error or an unlikely mistake in the physical manufacture of the bound volume, a copy of the Bible will be a perfect reproduction of the text which was presented to the printer. There is no possibility that an individual copy will differ from the text of the publisher's plates and that one's text of the Gospel of Mark will break off and be replaced, say, by a passage from *Alice in Wonderland* or *The Lord of the Rings.*

Before the invention of printing, however, copies of the Bible and all other books were produced by hand, and the possibility was greater that accidental or even intentional changes might be made in the text. The most recent stage in the manual copying of the Bible was during the Middle Ages, when the copyists were monks whose work was done under the supervision of the Church. Because the medieval scribes considered their work to be service to God, their copying was normally done quite accurately. Indeed, if the copying was done well, the scribe would have produced a perfect copy of his examplar.[11] Sometimes this ideal was approached very closely. Some manuscripts exist which had been copied by the same scribe, and are virtually identical word for word and letter for letter, and can be distinguished only by careful examination.

No matter how much care was taken, however, some errors were bound to have occurred. Sometimes, as with all human activities, fatigue or boredom set in, and the quality of the copy suffered as a result. If two consecutive lines of text began or ended with the same word, one of the lines may have been omitted by an inattentive scribe. Where two Greek letters were similar in their appearance, one may have been substituted for the other, especially if the substitution appeared to make sense in the context. (Not all medieval copyists would have received high marks for their penmanship.)

Before the copying of Bibles came under ecclesiastical control, a common way of reproducing manuscripts was for a reader to dictate the

---

11. The term "exemplar" is used for the manuscript from which a copy has been made. The more familiar term "original" is not appropriate, since the author's original manuscript may have been written over a thousand years earlier.

words of the text carefully to a group of writers in a *scriptorium,* each of whom would write down what he had heard. This method had the advantage of being able to produce multiple copies from a single reading of the exemplar, and was commonly used by commercial book manufacturers in the fourth century and later.

Although this method of producing copies by dictation was theoretically capable of producing perfect copies, the chances for error were greater than when a copy was individually written by a particular scribe. In Greek, as in English, many words sound the same as others with different meanings, and even some words which one reader would pronounce differently are indistinguishable when spoken by another. (Most Americans, for example, do not completely distinguish between the sounds of "merry," "Mary," and "marry," although which of these are pronounced similarly differs regionally.) While the production of manuscripts by dictation was quantitatively efficient, the quality of the Bibles produced was frequently poor.

At the earliest stage in the transmission of the Christian Bible, before Christianity had become an officially recognized religion in the Roman Empire and it had become commercially profitable to produce Bibles in quantity, the only way by which one could obtain a copy of the Bible was to copy it out for oneself or, more commonly, to pay someone else to make a copy. At its best, this way of reproducing the text was highly accurate. In practice, however, the earliest copyists were also subject to errors in correctly deciphering and transcribing the pages before them. In addition, economic factors tended to reduce the quality of their work. The medieval scribes, as we have seen, were monks whose work was part of their religious vocation. The earliest copyists were professionals who were customarily paid by the line rather than by the hour. A copyist who worked rapidly increased his income over that of a slower and more meticulous colleague. Since the incentive of these copyists was more economic than religious, their standards of accuracy were more pragmatic than ideal. The earliest copyings of the Bible were often therefore less accurate than those which would be done later in the Middle Ages.

Before modern methods of textual criticism were developed, the problem for the reader was that printed Bibles were based on medieval copies, which were produced, in turn, from earlier copies of still earlier manuscripts. The high standards of accuracy observed by the printer and the medieval scribe sometimes guaranteed only that a copy of the Bible would faithfully reproduce errors that had already occurred at an earlier stage in the reproduction of the text.[12]

The preceding paragraphs describe the textual situation of the New Testament which was copied by Christian scribes. The situation with regard to the Hebrew Old Testament is different in two important respects. The first is that there exist far fewer manuscripts of the Hebrew Old Testament than of the New Testament, and that those complete manuscripts that we do have are much more recent than the New Testament texts available to us. A second difference between the New and Old Testaments is that the copying of the Hebrew Old Testament remained under religious control during most if not all of the period during which the New Testament was being copied independently. The result is that higher standards of accuracy prevailed among Jewish than Christian scribes during the early centuries.[13] For these and other reasons, the problems and methods relating to the textual criticism of the Old Testament are in many ways considerably different from those which apply to the New Testament and are less accessible to the non-specialist. The remainder of the present chapter will therefore be limited to the textual criticism of the New Testament.

The Practice of Textual Criticism. The preceding paragraphs may have left the reader with an understandable sense of futility: since there are so many ways by which the original text of the New Testament may have been altered, what hope is there of reading the Bible with any assurance that one is reading what the author actually wrote? The modern science of textual criticism attempts to provide just this assur-

---

12. It will be recalled that one of the reasons for the revision of the venerable King James Version of the New Testament is that it was translated, with meticulous care, from a poor Greek text containing, in the words of the editors of the Revised Standard Version, "the accumulated errors of fourteen centuries of manuscript copying."

13. The discovery in 1947 among the Dead Sea Scrolls of a text of Isaiah that was a thousand years older than the medieval Hebrew manuscripts that were previously available provided evidence of the care taken by Jewish scribes during the intervening centuries.

ance by restoring, with a high degree of probability, the original wording of the New Testament. The remainder of this chapter will outline and illustrate the steps taken by textual scholars in restoring the text. A following section will discuss how the principles of textual criticism can be used by the reader who is not a biblical specialist.

The first step: collecting the evidence. The first step in investigating the text of a New Testament passage is to collect all available evidence relating to the text. Much of the work of collecting the manuscript evidence has already been done. Standard catalogues of Greek manuscripts exist, listing manuscripts, their dates, their contents, and the libraries in which they may be found. Newly-discovered manuscripts are described in the journals read by biblical scholars, such as the *Journal of Biblical Literature.* The readings of the manuscripts may be examined by means of a photographic copy, or by a collation found in a journal article or in a printed critical edition of the Greek New Testament.

Printed texts of the New Testament frequently cite manuscipts in groups rather than by individual witnesses. The reason for grouping manuscripts is in part a matter of convenience; since at least five thousand manuscripts of the New Testament are in existence, it is simply more efficient to cite them in groups rather than individually.[14] A more important reason, however, is that the number of manuscripts supporting a given reading is of almost no importance in determining the quality of the reading itself. A given early medieval manuscript may have been copied more frequently than another, or may have had more of its copies survive to be discovered by modern scholars, but this fact does not indicate that its text is superior to that of another ancient witness of which fewer copies exist today. By citing manuscripts in groups, attention is called to the quality of the manuscripts supporting a reading, and not to their number.

---

14. Kurt Aland's 1963 catalogue had 4,969 entries; by 1969 he reported that 300 additional witnesses should be added to this number. Jack Finnegan, *Encountering New Testament Manuscripts* (Grand Rapids: Eerdmans, 1974), p. 53.

The second step: evaluating the manuscripts. Before a judgment can be reached about a given reading, the manuscripts supporting it must be considered. The consideration of the manuscripts containing a reading is called "external evidence," as contrasted to the examination of the reading itself, or "internal evidence." Among the factors used in determining the reliability of a manuscript is its age. At 1 Corinthians 12:13, for example, the majority of manuscripts read, "We . . . all were made to drink of one Spirit." A variant reading is "We . . . all were made to drink of one drink." It is easy to see how this alteration occurred: the Greek word for "Spirit" is *pneuma,* whereas "drink" is *poma.* The likelihood of confusion is enhanced by the fact that *pneuma* was commonly abbreviated in uncial or block letters as ΠΜΑ, which closely resembles ΠΟΜΑ, *poma.* Once the alteration is explained, however, one must then determine the reading which is more likely to be correct. This is established in this case by noting that the most important manuscript supporting "drink" is from the twelfth century, whereas all the important earlier witnesses read "Spirit."

The third step: evaluating the reading. The contribution of external evidence is most frequently negative: it allows us to exclude from consideration readings which are attested only in late or in otherwise unreliable manuscripts. Frequently, however, manuscripts of approximately equal reliability will differ among themselves. This is the case with regard to the phrase "the Son of God" in Mark 1:1, which has been described above. In such instances, a final decision about the readings must be made on the basis of "internal evidence," evidence derived from an examination of the readings themselves.

The most important criterion in the use of internal evidence is based on a knowledge of the most common scribal errors. Since scribes are more likely to incorporate marginal glosses and other additions into the text than they are to omit material, a standard principle is that the shorter of two readings is often the more likely to be correct. An instance of preferring the shorter reading is Romans 8:1, in which the majority of manuscripts read, "There is therefore now no condemnation for those who are in Christ Jesus, who do not walk in the manner of the flesh but in the manner of the Spirit." A shorter reading omits the final phrase, and ends with "Christ Jesus." This variation cannot be decided on the basis of the manuscripts supporting each reading: Codex Vaticanus[15] and the original text of Sinaiticus support the shorter reading, while the longer reading (or a variation of it) is supported by Alexandrinus and the corrected reading of Sinaiticus. The question becomes clear, however, by asking the questions, "If the longer reading had not been in the original, why would a scribe have added it?" and "If the longer reading had been in the original, why would a scribe have left it out?" There are ample reasons why the longer reading may have been added to the text; such observations about Christian life-styles are typical of devotional comments or glosses. There are, on the other hand, no good reasons why a scribe would have intentionally omitted the longer version if it had been in the original. The tendency among scribes was to omit nothing considered to be sacred, and there is nothing in the additional phrase to have motivated a copyist to delete it from his text.[16] The case against the longer reading is made certain in this case by the observation that the added words were copied from the third verse following. An early commentator had used the phrase in his marginal gloss on 8:1, and it became a part of the text.

A second criterion used in determining internal evidence is based on the observation that scribal changes were usually in the direction of clarifying obscure details in the text rather than of making them less intelligible. (This criterion obviously applies in cases where alternative readings both make sense; a spelling error is recognizable as such.) Such a "correction" has taken place in many manuscripts of Mark 1:2, where a quotation from both Malachi 3:1 and Isaiah 40:3 is introduced with the words, "As it is written in Isaiah the prophet." Since the citation in fact combines quotations from two prophets of whom Isaiah was not even the first, the majority of manuscripts have changed this introductory

---

15. The term "codex" denotes a manuscript which is in the form of a volume of pages like a modern book, rather than in the form of a scroll. The convenience of a bound volume over a roll led to its adoption by Christian scribes as early as the second century.

16. The thought that might occur to the modern reader, that the phrase about not walking in the manner of the flesh might have been omitted by a scribe who objected to such restrictions on his life-style, is not to the point: a monk living an ascetic life would have been pleased rather than offended by the longer reading, since it supported his vocation.

phrase to read, "As it is written in the prophets."[17] The governing principle is that in general the more difficult reading is to be preferred.

Illustrating the Principles of Textual Criticism. The preceding pages have briefly described the principles of textual criticism as they are employed by biblical scholars. These techniques are not generally employable by the general reader. Some require linguistic and other training that the non-specialist will not possess. The study of which manuscripts support a given reading, for instance, requires the ability to use a critical edition of the Greek New Testament. In addition, many of the textual problems have been solved to such a degree of assurance that, in the absence of new manuscript evidence, no further consideration is necessary. Modern translations of the New Testament employ the work of textual scholars and are made from the best critical texts which can be established. It may interest the reader, however, to illustrate how these principles are employed by scholars. Three cases will be examined in the following paragraphs.

1. *The Case of John 5:2–5.* The Revised Standard Version of John 5:2–5 reads:

> 2 Now there is in Jerusalem by the Sheep Gate a pool, in Hebrew called Bethzatha, [j] which has five porticoes. 3 In these lay a multitude of invalids, blind, lame, paralyzed.[k] 5 One man was there, who had been ill for thirty-eight years.

The small superscript letters refer to the following footnotes:

> [j] Other ancient authorities read *Bethesda*, others *Bethsaida*.
> [k] Other ancient authorities insert, wholly or in part, *waiting for the moving of the water: 4 for an angel of the Lord went down at certain seasons into the pool, and troubled the water: whoev-*

---

17. One scholar has observed, "Odd though it may seem, scribes who thought were more dangerous than those who wished merely to be faithful in copying what lay before them. Many of the alterations which may be classified as intentional were no doubt introduced in good faith by copyists who believed that they were correcting an error or infelicity of language which had previously crept into the sacred text and needed to be rectified": Bruce M. Metzger, *The Text of the New Testament* (New York: Oxford University Press, 1968), p. 195.

er stepped in first after the troubling of the water was healed of whatever disease he had.

Thus, there are two textual variations in this passage. The first, concerning the Hebrew or Aramaic name of the pool, relates to the problem of rendering a name from one language into another language using a different alphabet, and need not concern us further. It is the second variant which is the more interesting. The shorter reading found in the Revised Standard Version text simply locates the handicapped persons at the pool by the Sheep Gate; the longer reading found in the footnote explains why they are there.

Of interest to the scholar is the question of which manuscripts support each of these readings. This information is found in a critical edition of the Greek New Testament, and is not printed in the notes to translations of the Bible. In most instances where external evidence is decisive, however, most recent translations employ the best reading without noting the existence of variations. The appearance of a textual footnote usually means that the matter cannot be settled on external evidence alone.

The first principle of internal evidence described above was that the shorter reading is the more likely to be correct. This is because the scribe is more likely to add to his text, either by way of explanation or by the accidental inclusion of a marginal gloss, than he is to omit material found before him. The questions to be asked in the case of John 5:2–5 are the following: "If the original text did not include the longer reading, is there a reason why a copyist would have added it?" "If the longer reading were a part of the original text, is there a reason to explain how it would have been omitted?" The first question is surely the easier to answer: the shorter reading virtually begs the question of why this assembly of invalids was gathered at the pool in the first place. Was the pool by the Sheep Gate a part of an ancient nursing facility? Was it a spa of sorts where people gathered for their health? The ancient scribe as well as the modern reader was led to infer that the people were at the pool somehow because of their handicaps, because they believed that in some way their conditions might be improved by their presence there. From making this inference it is only a short step to the creation of a pious explanation about an angel, and to the incorporation of this legend into the text. There is, on the other hand, no good reason why such an explanation would have been omitted by the scribe if it had once been a part of the account. However the modern reader may be jarred by the account of an occasional angelic miracle, no medieval copyist would have omitted the longer reading on this account. The shorter reading is therefore the more likely to be original.[18]

2. *The Case of Luke 3:22.* The Revised Standard Version of Luke 3:22 concludes the narrative of Jesus' baptism with the following words:

> . . . and a voice came from heaven, "Thou art my beloved Son;[j] with thee I am well pleased.[k]

The footnotes to this verse are:

> [j] Or, *my Son, my* (or *the*) *Beloved.*
> [k] Other ancient authorities read *today I have begotten thee.*

The first footnote describes an alternative way to translate the Greek text: *ho huios mou ho agapētos* may be translated either "my beloved Son" or "my Son, the Beloved." The second note describes a textual variant that will warrant our consideration.

The textual variation in Luke 3:22 is between those manuscripts which have the heavenly voice say to Jesus, ". . . with thee I am well pleased," and those reading, ". . . today I have begotten thee." In Greek as in English, the lengths of the two readings differ by only one word, so the principle of preferring the shorter reading will not offer much assistance. (In Greek, however, the "well-pleased" reading is the shorter.) The applicable principle in this case is that of preferring the reading which is the more difficult, and which the scribe is more likely to have altered in favor of the other.

---

18. In the present case an indication of the scribes' inclination to add explanations to the text is the Revised Standard Version's statement that the longer reading is found in some authorities "wholly or in part." A preliminary level of explanation may have been that the water was believed to be curative as a result of some natural phenomenon. A later addition raised this natural explanation to the supernatural level by inserting the statement about the angel.

The questions to be addressed in the case of Luke 3:22 are: "On the one hand, if the 'begotten' reading were original, why would a copyist have changed it to read 'well pleased'?" "On the other hand, if 'well pleased' stood in the original text, is there a reason why a scribe would have substituted 'begotten'?" A preliminary observation in the present instance is that the "more difficult" reading need not present insurmountable obstacles to the copyist. There is nothing to trouble a scribe in stating that Jesus was pleasing to God, nor in speaking of him as the begotten of his Father. In this case as in others, therefore, the "more difficult" reading is to be identified not because of its intrinsic problems, but because of the attractiveness of the alternative.

A clue to which reading was the more attractive to the scribe is found in the cross-references to Luke 3:22. The most interesting of these for the present purpose is the reference to Psalm 2:7. The second psalm is a royal psalm, used on the occasion of the installation of a king. Its seventh verse reads:

> I will tell of the decree of the LORD: He said to me, "You are my son, today I have begotten you."

Once it is discovered that the "begotten" reading is in fact a quotation from the second psalm, the questions about the readings can be put in this form: "If the original text of Luke 3:22 quoted from Psalm 2:7 in reference to Jesus, why would this reference have been omitted by a scribe?" "If, on the other hand, the original text read 'well pleased,' why would this have been changed to an Old Testament quotation?" The relative attractiveness of the two readings now becomes apparent. The early Christians commonly cited Old Testament passages which seemed to them to describe or to predict events in the life of Jesus. If, on the one hand, Luke 3:22 had originally read "begotten," there is no explanation why this Old Testament allusion would have been deleted by a copyist. If, on the other hand, the original text had been "Thou art my beloved Son; with thee I am well pleased," it is clear how the opening would have called Psalm 2:7 to the mind of the scribe, who then completed the sentence, ". . . today I have begotten thee." While neither reading of Luke 3:22 is intrinsically difficult, the more attractive reading is surely "begotten," and therefore "well pleased" is to be identified as the relatively more difficult original.[19]

3. *The Case of Matthew 24:36.* The variant reading at Matthew 24:36 is one in which the conclusions from the criteria diverge and in which a determination can only be obtained by balancing the several factors. Chapters 24 and 25 of Matthew are a series of sayings by Jesus about the end of the age and the judgment. In the Revised Standard Version of Matthew 24:36, Jesus says:

36 "But of that day and hour no one knows, not even the angels of heaven, nor the Son,[a] but the Father only."

The footnote to this verse is:

[a] Other ancient authorities omit *nor the Son.*

The questions to be asked about this verse are: "On the one hand, if 'nor the Son' was not in Matthew's original text, why would a scribe have added it?" "On the other hand, if these words were omitted by the scribe, why would he have done so?" At first consideration, the situation appears to be one in which a scribe has added to the text, perhaps by incorporating a marginal gloss of some kind. If this were the case, the problem of the text would be expected to yield to the criterion of preferring the shorter reading.

The second criterion which we have been observing is that of preferring the more difficult reading. One way in which scribes created less difficult readings was to harmonize Gospel narratives with parallels in other Gospels. A parallel passage to Matthew 24:36 is found in Mark 13:32, which reads, "But of that day or that hour no one knows, not even the angels in heaven, nor the Son, but only the Father." This verse is virtually identical to the longer reading of Matthew 24:36, and is read by virtually all manuscripts, including those containing the shorter

---

19. Psalm 2:7 is also applied to Jesus in Acts 13:33 and Hebrews 1:5. A scribe familiar with these passages would have been even more likely to have introduced an allusion to Psalm 2:7 into Luke 3:22.

reading in Matthew. If a scribe had been thinking of the passage in Mark while he was copying Matthew, the absence of "nor the Son" from Matthew might have seemed defective, and the longer reading might have seemed created to harmonize the passage with the parallel in Mark. Since it did not harmonize as well, the shorter reading would also have been the more difficult reading.

It is more likely, however, that in the present instance the difficulty which led to emendation of the text was theological instead of literary. In Matthew 24:36 Jesus is talking about ignorance: no one, not even the angels, knows when the end will come. To include the longer reading in Matthew 24:36 is to include Jesus among those who are ignorant. (In good company, perhaps, with the angels, but ignorant still!) It is much more likely that the longer reading, which seemed to imply ignorance on the part of Jesus, was written into the text by the original author than that it was added later by a Christian scribe. While it is in principle possible for the words "nor the Son" to have been a harmonistic addition, it is more likely that their absence in other manuscripts was a scribal omission in the interest of orthodox theology. Merrill M. Parvis has noted that scribes were interested not in the "original reading" but in the "true reading."[20] If harmonistic and theological considerations conflicted, it is the theological which was more likely to have induced changes in the text. In the case of Matthew 24:36, most modern scholars are persuaded in favor of the longer reading, and this reading is found in the Jerusalem, New American, and Today's English Bibles, as well as the Revised Standard Version.

Textual Criticism and the General Reader. Some of the textual notes in modern Bibles call attention to readings which appear in the King James Version but which have now been rejected by almost all scholars. Other notes, however, report textual difficulties which have not yet been solved with complete assurance. In some cases, such as that of John 2:2–5, the original text can be determined with a high degree of certainty. In other cases, including that which we have examined in

---

20. "Text, NT," *The Interpreter's Dictionary of the Bible* (Nashville: Abingdon, 1962), Vol. 4, p. 595.

Matthew 24:36, the applicable criteria seem to offset one another, and we can speak only of a greater or a lesser degree of probability.[21] The purpose of this portion of this chapter is to illustrate how the principles of textual criticism are employed by those who have been trained in their use. The general reader may wish to apply these principles in evaluating the various readings which are indicated by the footnotes in his or her Bible. In so doing, however, one should not assume that he or she has actually solved those textual dilemmas which remain opaque to those with resources which the non-specialist is not likely to possess.

A second observation is perhaps in order: The most important teachings of the Bible are found throughout its pages, and are not confined to a few isolated verses. In using the Bible for one's own theological or ethical guidance, therefore, it is perhaps best to be conservative in matters relating to the text, and to avoid basing one's most important conclusions on passages where a high degree of textual certainty is lacking.

The present chapter has introduced and illustrated the practice of the textual criticism of the New Testament and demonstrated how the principles of textual study may be understood by the general reader. Since the chapter is about errors in the text and their detection, it is appropriate to conclude with a reminder of the care taken by the majority of scribes. The following words from the conclusion of the Book of Revelation may have been intended as a warning to copyists:

> I warn everyone who hears the words of the prophecy of this book: if any one adds to them, God will add to him the plagues described in this book, and if any one takes away from the words of the book of this prophecy, God will take away his share in the tree of life and in the holy city, which are described in this book (22:18–19).

Most scribes took such warnings and their work seriously. The largest number of the errors which did occur as the results of lapses in the

---

21. The editors of the United Bible Societies' *Greek New Testament* print the longer reading in their text but indicate that considerable doubt exists as to whether it or the shorter reading is superior.

copyists' care are singular or minority readings and are easily detected by specialists. The relatively few problems that do remain, and which are noted in the Revised Standard Version and other modern translations, are often interesting and challenging, but almost never vital to Christian religion or to life.

QVATVOR EVANGELIA, AD VETVSTISSIMORVM EXEMPLARIVM LATINORVM FIDEM, ET AD GRAECAM VERITATEM AB ERASMO ROTE RODAMO SACRAE THEOLOGIAE PROFES SORE DILIGENTER RECOGNITA.

ΕΥΑΓΓΕΛΙΟΝ ΚΑΤΑ ΜΑΤΘΑΙΟΝ.

ΙΒΛΟΣ γενέσεως ΙΗΣΧΡΙΣΤΟΥ, ἡοῦ Δαβίδ, ἡοῦ ἀβραάμ. Αβραὰμ ἐγέννησεν τ ἰσαάκ. ἰσαὰκ ἢ, ἐγέννησεν τὸν ἰακώβ. ἰακώβ δὲ, ἐγέννησεν τὸν ἰούδαν, καὶ τοὺς ἀδελφοὺς αὐτοῦ. ἰούδας δὲ, ἐγέννησεν τὸν φαρὲς, ὶ τὸν ζαρὰ, ἐκ τῆ θάμαρ. φαρὲς δὲ, ἐγέννησεν τ ἐσρώμ. ἐσρώμ δὲ, ἐγέννησεν τὸν ἀράμ. ἀρὰμ δὲ ἐγέννησεν τὸν ἀμιναδάβ. ἀμιναδὰβ δὲ, ἐγέννησεν τ ναασσόρ. ναασσὸρ δὲ, ἐγέννησεν τ σαλμών. σαλμὼν ἢ, ἐγέννησεν τ βοὸζ ἐκ τῆ ῥαχάβ. βοὸζ ἢ, ἐγέννησεν τὸν ὠβὴδ, ἐκ τῆ ῥούθ. ὠβὴδ ἢ, ἐγέννησεν τὸν ἰεσσαί. ἰεσσαὶ δὲ, ἐγέννησεν τὸν δαβὶδ τὸν βασιλέα. Δαβὶδ ἢ ὁ βασιλεὺς ἐγέννησεν τὸν σολομῶνα ἐκ τῆ τοῦ οὐρίου. σολομὼν δὲ, ἐγέννησεν τ ῥοβοάμ. ῥοβοὰμ ἢ, ἐγέννησεν τὸν ἀβιὰ. ἀβιὰ δὲ, ἐγέννησεν τ ἀσά. ἀσὰ ἢ, ἐγέννησεν τὸν ἰωσαφάτ. ἰωσαφὰτ ἢ, ἐγέννησεν τὸν ἰωράμ. ἰωρὰμ ἢ, ἐγέν νησεν τὸν

EVANGELIVM SECVNDVM MATTHAEVM.

Iber generationis Iesu Christi filij Dauid, Filij Abrahã, Abraham genuit Isaâc. Isaac aũt, genuit Iacob. Iacob aũt, genuit Iudã, & fratres eius. Iudas aũt, genuit Phares, & Zarã, e Thamar. Phares autẽ, genuit Esrom. Esrom aũt, genuit Aram. Arã autem, genuit Aminadab. Aminadab aũt, genuit Naasson. Naasson aũt, genuit Salmon. Salmon autẽ, genuit Boos, e Rhachab. Boos aũt, genuit Obed, e Ruth. Obed autẽ, genuit Iesse, Iesse aũt, genuit Dauid regem. Dauid autẽ rex, genuit Solomonem, ex ea q̃ fuerat uxor Vrie. Solomon autem, genuit Roboam. Roboam aũt, genuit Abiam. Abia autem, genuit Asa. Asa autem, genuit Iosaphat. Iosaphat autem, genuit Ioram. Ioram autem, genuit Oziã.

A

IOANNES FROBENIVS SVIS TYPIS EXCVDEBAT

4

Interpreting the Bible

A large portion of the material in the preceding three chapters has been of an historical nature. We have seen how Protestant and Catholic Christians have defined their canons of scriptural writings. We have looked at the history of the translation of the Bible and have seen how several modern translations came to be made. We have observed how manuscripts of the Bible were copied at different times in the history of Christianity. When Christians have read the Bible, however, their interest has usually not been historical. What the religious reader of the Bible usually seeks is not information about the past but guidance for the present. If the Bible is viewed as a document of history, it is not that its religious reader seeks to enter the past as an historical investigator, but that he or she anticipates that the message which was heard in the past will continue to guide people today. The statement found in 2 Timothy 3:16–17 is characteristic of the religious attitude toward the Bible:

> All scripture is inspired by God and profitable for teaching, for reproof, for correction, and for training in righteousness, that the man of God may be complete, equipped for every good work.

When the Bible is seen as providing something which is profitable to the reader, an important question is how one is to read it in order to understand its message. The term for the process by which one seeks to understand the Bible is derived from the Greek verb *hermēneuō,* which means "to explain" or "to interpret."One's method of interpreting the

Bible is called one's "hermeneutic"; the plural noun, "hermeneutics," denotes the systematic study of methods of biblical interpretation.

It is important to understand that all who seek guidance from the Bible have a hermeneutic, a method of interpretation. In some cases their method of understanding the text has been carefully thought through and clearly expressed. Some biblical scholars have given a great deal of attention to matters of hermeneutics and have written textbooks on the interpretation and theological use of the Bible. More frequently, however, one's hermeneutic may be unconscious and unexamined. If a contemporary reader randomly opens the Bible in search of a message for the day, he or she has already made the hermeneutical assumption that in some way related to God's illumination or to his or her own imagination the ancient text will have something to say today. The difference between the ancient rabbis, who interpreted passages grammatically on the principle that "the Torah speaks the language of men," and those modern readers who let their Bibles fall open haphazardly in search of a "daily verse," is not that the former have a hermeneutic while the latter do not.[1] Both sets of readers have made hermeneutical assumptions. The difference between them is in the nature of their respective assumptions and, most likely, in whether they are aware of what their hermeneutical assumptions and principles might be. As much as the statements, "I have looked up all the passages on this subject, and I think that. . . ." and "I prayed for guidance, and the Lord showed me. . . ." may differ in their hermeneutical assumptions, these are both hermeneutical statements, since they both reveal the principles underlying their speakers' conclusions. The present chapter will examine several of the ways by which the Bible has been understood from the early centuries of Christianity until the present, and will outline the development of Christian hermeneutical methods.

---

1. There is a famous and, one hopes, apocryphal story about an individual who opened his Bible three times in search of guidance on a given morning and was increasingly disconcerted to happen on the sentences, "And he went and hanged himself" (Matthew 27:5), "Go and do likewise" (Luke 10:37), and "What you are going to do, do quickly" (John 13:27).

Biblical Interpretation in the Time of Jesus

Several different methods of biblical interpretation were in use in the first century. These methods were derived from the practice of making homiletical expansions upon the text in the synagogue, from the need of the various religious sects to corroborate the truth of their beliefs by appealing to the commonly-held Jewish Scriptures, and from the practice of observing minute details in the biblical text as a means of applying the Bible to matters of Jewish law.

The Targum. By the time of Jesus, the common language of Judea and several other areas of the Near East was Aramaic. This was a semitic language which was similar to Hebrew, and which had come to be spoken throughout a large region as the official language of the Persian empire. After the Persians had been conquered by Alexander the Great, several dialects of Aramaic continued to be spoken as the language of the people. Among those who continued to speak Aramaic were the Jews of Judea. A religious problem was created by the use of Aramaic as the vernacular among Jews because the Hebrew Scriptures, which were read aloud in the synagogue services, had become unintelligible to their hearers. Since one of the functions of the synagogue was that of instruction, it became customary to supplement the Hebrew reading with a translation or paraphrase into the common Aramaic. This supplement was called a *targum,* which was the Hebrew word for "translation."

Some scholars believe that the practice of rendering the Hebrew reading into the Aramaic vernacular began as long ago as the time of Ezra in the fifth century B.C., and that such a translation is attested in Nehemiah 8:7–8.

> The Levites helped the people to understand the law, while the people remained in their places. And they read from the book, from the law of God, clearly; and they gave the sense, so that the people understood the meaning.

Although targums were originally made extemporaneously to accompany the readings in the synagogue, they eventually came to have a fixed written form. Aramaic targums were known to the rabbis of the first century, and fragments of targums on Leviticus and on Job have been found among the Dead Sea Scrolls. Targumic interpretations were known to Essenes, Pharisees, and to the early Christians, and cannot be associated with any one movement.

The distinction between a translation and a sermon was often not observed in the making of a targum, and passages in the targums frequently include sermonic expansions of the Hebrew text. As an example, we may examine an interpretation of Genesis 3:14–15 which explains the fact that people usually dislike snakes:

> The LORD God said to the serpent ". . . I will put enmity between you and the woman, and between your seed and her seed; he shall bruise your head, and you shall bruise his heel."

The concern of the passage to Targum Pseudo-Jonathan, however, is not biological but ethical and theological. The targum identifies the serpent as Satan (an identification which is not made at all in the Hebrew text), and renders the passage:

> And I will put enmity between you and the woman between the descendants of your sons and the descendants of her sons. And it shall come to pass when the sons of the woman keep the precepts of the Law, they shall aim at you and smite you on the head. But when they forsake the precepts of the Law you shall aim at them and bite them on their heels. For them, however, there will be a remedy. And they are to effect a crushing in the end, in the days of King Messiah.[2]

This interpretation may have been known to Paul, who wrote in Romans 16:19–20:

---

2. Martin McNamara, *Targum and Testament* (Grand Rapids, Mich.: Eerdmans, 1972), p. 121.

I would have you wise as to what is good and guileless as to what is evil; then the God of peace will soon crush Satan under your feet.

For both Pseudo-Jonathan and Paul, the deeds of the righteous will crush Satan in the coming days of the kingdom of God.

In another example, Targum Neofiti paraphrases Genesis 1:3–5, which reads:

And God said, "Let there be light"; and there was light. And God saw that the light was good; and God separated the light from the darkness. God called the light Day, and darkness he called Night. And there was evening and there was morning, one day.

A problem which sometimes occurs to the reader of Genesis is that we are told that the sun and the moon were not created until the fourth day of creation (Genesis 1:14–19). How then could there be light on the first day? Targum Neofiti offers the following explanation:

The earth was void and empty and darkness was spread over the face of the abyss. And the Word of the Lord was the light and it shone; and he called it the first night.[3]

The difficulty is resolved: it is the Word of the Lord, and not the sun and the moon, which was the source of the light. The targum's expansion of the Hebrew text may have been known to the author of the Gospel of John who associated the Word of God with light in John 1:1–5:

In the beginning was the Word, and the Word was with God, and the Word was God. . . . In him was life, and the life was the light of men. The light shines in the darkness, and the darkness has not overcome it.

---

3. *Ibid.,* p. 103.

There is some disagreement among biblical scholars about the extent of the influence of the targums on the writers of the New Testament. It is not necessary to suppose that Paul and John were actually copying from Pseudo-Jonathan and Neofiti to recognize that the biblical interpretations which are preserved in the targums were also known to the authors of the New Testament. By shedding light on the background to the New Testament, the targums have allowed scholars to understand the development of early Christian theology.

Jewish Typology. The typological method of Jewish biblical interpretation is sometimes known by the Hebrew word *pesher,* which meant "interpretation." It was usually in the form of a commentary on a biblical text, in which the text was read as though it were a prophecy referring to the time of the commentator. Several of the Dead Sea Scrolls preserve commentaries on the writings of the Old Testament prophets. An example may be taken from a commentary on Habakkuk 2:2. This verse reads:

And the Lord answered me: "Write the vision; make it plain upon tablets, so that he may run who reads it."

The commentator, who is an Essene, understands the passage to refer, not to the time of the prophet, but to the time of the founder of his own sect centuries later:

And God told Habakkuk to write down that which would happen to the final generation, but He did not make known to him when time would end. And as for that which He said, *That he who reads it may read it speedily,* interpreted this concerns the Teacher of Righteousness, to whom God made known all the mysteries of the words of his servants the prophets.[4]

---

4. Geza Vermes, *The Dead Sea Scrolls in English* (Baltimore: Penguin Books, 1968), p. 239.

The Essene commentator believes that he understands what the prophets themselves did not, since their Teacher was taught the meaning of the Scriptures by God.

A second Essene example of Jewish typology is found in a Dead Sea commentary on Psalm 37:32–33, which reads:

> The wicked watches the righteous, and seeks to slay him. The LORD will not abandon him to his power, or let him be condemned when he is brought to trial.

The point of this passage is that God will vindicate persons who are righteous. The psalmist is not thinking of any particular righteous individual: singular and plural terms for the righteous alternate throughout the psalm. The Essene commentator, however, takes the passage to be a prophecy of the Teacher of Righteousness who was persecuted by his enemies:

> Interpreted, this concerns the Wicked Priest who rose up against the Teacher of Righteousness that he might put him to death. . . . But God *will not abandon him into his hand and will not let him be condemned when he is tried.* And God will pay [the Wicked Priest] his reward by delivering him into the hand of the violent of the nations, that they may execute upon him the judgment of wickedness.[5]

The commentator has interpreted a general reference as though it were intended to be specific, and reads it as a prophecy of the life of the founder of his sect.

Typological interpretation was often employed by the early Christians as they read Old Testament passages which seemed to them to foreshadow or to predict events in the life of Jesus. The Gospel of Matthew in particular frequently cites the Old Testament in this way. An example is this Gospel's use of Isaiah 40:3, which reads:

---

5. *Ibid.,* p. 245.

> A voice cries: "In the wilderness prepare the way of the LORD, make straight in the desert a highway for our God."

This verse is part of the prophet's vision of the return of Jewish exiles from Babylon. The voice is the voice of God, establishing the highway through the wilderness upon which the Lord will triumphantly return with his people. The author of the Gospel, however, is not thinking of the events of the sixth century B.C. when he writes Matthew 3:1–3:

> In those days came John the Baptist, preaching in the wilderness of Judea, "Repent, for the kingdom of heaven is at hand." For this is he who was spoken of by the prophet Isaiah when he said, "The voice of one crying in the wilderness: 'Prepare the way of the Lord, make his paths straight.' "[6]

Since the coming of Jesus is even more important to Matthew than the return of the exiles, he reads Isaiah so that the voice *concerning* the wilderness becomes the heralding cry *in* the wilderness of the forerunner of the messiah.

As we have observed in these examples, the typological method of interpretation characteristically interprets an ancient biblical passage as though it were a reference to the time of the interpreter. The original setting of the passage is usually ignored, and the interpreter often reads a general statement as though it were a specific reference. The interpreter is not really interested in the historical meaning of a biblical passage, since he believes that he is living in the time to which all the Scriptures point.[7] He and the members of his community have received the truth by God's revelation to their founder, and the typological meth-

---

6. Modern quotation marks did not exist in the first century, so Matthew's reading of Isaiah is not an unwarranted interpretation of the original, which was like "A voice cries in the wilderness prepare the way of the Lord."

7. A near relative of the typology which one occasionally finds in theological disputes is the practice of proof-texting, in which one combs the Bible for passages in support of one's position, with little regard to their meaning in their original context. Occasionally a similar treatment of the Bible is heard in sermons, when a passage is used as the springboard for the comments of the preacher. The observation that this method reads into a passage an idea derived elsewhere applies as well to these contemporary situations.

od is the way by which the ancient text is read as a sort of confirmation of that which has been revealed. Since he believes that the coming of his founder—whether the Essene Teacher or Jesus—is the most important event in human history, it would have been literally inconceivable to the typological commentator that the passages he cited could have been intended to mean something else. However we might evaluate this method of interpretation today, its use enabled the early Christians to see Jesus as the fulfillment of the Old Testament, and therefore to understand Christianity not as a departure from the past, but as a movement in essential continuity with that which God had already done.

Jewish Literal Exegesis. In its most general sense, the term "Jewish exegesis," like its Hebrew equivalent *midrash,* may be used to describe any of the methods of biblical interpretation which were used by the rabbis of the first and later centuries. In the present context, as "Jewish *literal* exegesis," the term is used in a more restricted sense to denote the hermeneutical method which was characterized by attention to textual, grammatical, and linguistic details and which was formulated into specific interpretative principles during the first and second centuries.

The first person to be identified as having formulated specific rules for interpreting the Bible was Rabbi Hillel, who lived from about 50 B.C. to about 10 A.D. As a Pharisee, Hillel sought to use the Bible as a source of Jewish law and a guide to conduct. It was for this purpose that he presented the following hermeneutical principles: (1) inferring from the less important to the more important, (2) inferring on the basis of wording, (3) establishing a general rule on the basis of one passage, (4) establishing a general rule on the basis of two passages, (5) reasoning from the particular to the general and from the general to the particular, (6) interpreting by means of another similar passage, and (7) deducing from the context. These principles probably were not invented by Hillel, and it is possible that they were derived from the methods which had been used by Greek scholars in interpreting the Greek classics. The effect of these principles, which were refined by later rabbis, was to establish a method of understanding a biblical text which was based on a careful examination of the details of the text itself. The formulation of the principles of literal exegesis was unique to Pharisaism, and it is in the writings of the Pharisees that the most instances of its use are found.

An example of the use of this method is found in a second-century collection of legal commentary on the Book of Numbers called *Midrash Sifre.* One of the passages discussed is Numbers 15:32–33:

> While the people of Israel were in the wilderness, they found a man gathering sticks on the sabbath day. And those who found him gathering sticks on the sabbath day brought him to Moses and Aaron, and to all the congregation.

The rabbis observed that the passage states twice that the offender had been gathering sticks on the Sabbath. Since nothing in the Bible can be thought to be meaningless, the repetition of this detail must have a significance. The *Midrash Sifre* comments:

> Why is it repeated? It implies that the man had been warned beforehand concerning works of this kind that are prohibited on the Sabbath. Hence the rule ... that a warning must be given first if the person breaking them is to be punished.[8]

The contemporary reader may disagree with the rabbis that this is the meaning of this passage. It is characteristic of this method, however, that details of this kind are observed and considered important for understanding the text.

Literal exegesis was occasionally used by the early Christians. The clearest example in the New Testament is perhaps Galatians 3:16, where Paul argues a theological point on the basis of a grammatically singular noun in Genesis 12:7. Paul's text of the latter verse read:

> Then the LORD appeared to Abram, and said, "To your offspring I will give this land."[9]

---

8. Howard Clark Kee, *The Origins of Christianity* (Englewood Cliffs, N.J.: Prentice-Hall, 1973), p. 136.

9. The Revised Standard Version reads, "To your descendants...." I have rendered the term as "offspring" to preserve the grammatical feature on which Paul's argument is based. The form, "Abram," is a shorter form of "Abraham."

The Hebrew word for "offspring," and its Greek equivalent in the Septuagint version which Paul was more likely to have consulted, is grammatically singular, although it can have a collective meaning. Paul's argument in Galatians is based on observing its grammatical number:

> Now the promises were made to Abraham and to his offspring. It does not say, "And to offsprings," referring to many; but, referring to one, "And to your offspring," which is Christ.

As we shall see below, the later Christian Church moved away from a literal approach to the Bible and came to interpret it metaphorically. When a hermeneutic employing a literal interpretation of the grammatical, lexical, and other details of the text eventually began to reappear in Christianity, this was the result of contacts between Christian scholars and the rabbis who had continued to practice Jewish literal exegesis. Thus, although this method is not used in its original form by Christian scholars, its preservation in the synagogue enabled it to become one of the forerunners of modern methods of Christian biblical study.

Biblical Interpretation in Later Christianity

As the Christian movement entered the Greek and Roman world, it initially perceived itself to be an alien movement in the midst of its Hellenistic setting. Among the factors which encouraged the early Christians to think of themselves in this way was the apocalyptic attitude that the present world is transitory, to be replaced some day by the kingdom of God. Perhaps a more important factor was the social status of most of the early Christians. Mostly members of the disadvantaged classes, they were outsiders sociologically as well as religiously, and many may have adopted the new faith as a way of attaining alternative comforts to those which were for them unattainable in the Roman system.[10] One aspect of society in which the early Christians clearly did

---

10. An important contribution to understanding the sociology of early Christianity is John Gager's *Kingdom and Community: The Social World of Early Christianity* (Englewood Cliffs, N.J.: Prentice-Hall, 1975).

not participate was the intellectual life of Hellenistic culture. Excluded from participation, the early Christians identified Greek learning with unbelief and their own rustic simplicity with pious virtue. The common Christian attitude can already be seen in 1 Corinthians 1:18–21:

> For the word of the cross is folly to those who are perishing, but to us who are being saved it is the power of God. For it is written, "I will destroy the wisdom of the wise, and the cleverness of the clever I will thwart." Where is the wise man? Where is the scribe? Where is the debater of this age? Has not God made foolish the wisdom of the world? For since, in the wisdom of God, the world did not know God, it pleased God through the folly of what we preach to save those who believe.

A similar attitude was expressed at the end of the second century by the Christian Tertullian:

> What is there in common between Athens and Jerusalem? What between the Academy and the Church? . . . After Christ Jesus we desire no subtle theories, no acute enquiries after the gospel.[11]

Other Christians, however, were prepared to enlist the categories of Greek learning in the service of the faith. Justin Martyr, who had received a Greek education before his conversion to Christianity in the second century, could identify "the Word" of John 1:1–14 with the *logos,* the divine rationality spoken of by the Stoic philosophers, and could write:

> We are taught that Christ is the first-born of God, and we have shown above that He is the reason of whom the whole human race partake. . . . Whatever has been uttered aright by any men in any place belongs to us Christians; for, next to God, we worship and love the reason which is from the unbegotten and

---

11. *De praescriptione haereticorum,* vii, in Henry Bettenson, ed., *Documents of the Christian Church* (London: Oxford University Press, 1963), p. 8.

ineffable God; since on our account He has been made man, that, being made partaker of our sufferings, he may also bring us healing.[12]

As philosophically-trained persons began to enter the Christian movement in the second and later centuries, they brought with them Hellenistic methods of interpreting sacred texts. In accepting and refining these methods the Christian Church developed the hermeneutics which were to serve it until the development of modern biblical study.

The Allegorical Method. One of the first Christians to present specific principles of biblical interpretation was Origen during the early third century, who wrote:

> I will endeavor to show what the accepted methods of interpretation are, and therefore I will follow the rule which has always been used in Jesus Christ's heavenly Church since the time of the Apostles.[13]

The hermeneutic which Origen presents, however, was derived not from the earliest Christians but from the method used by Greek scholars in interpreting the Homeric classics. The term "allegory" comes from the Greek verb *allēgoreō,* "to speak allegorically," and denotes a genre of speech or writing in which the intended meaning is conveyed metaphorically and in which the details of the account are to be understood as symbols rather than in their normal sense. The best-known allegory in English is John Bunyan's *The Pilgrim's Progress,* in which the experi-

---

12. *Apology* I. xliv. 2; II. xiii. r, in Bettenson, *Documents,* pp. 6–7. The Greek term *logos,* which was used for "Word" in John 1, had been used earlier by the Stoic philosophers to denote reason, which they thought to be a divine manifestation in man. There has been considerable controversy among scholars as to whether the usage in John 1 is derived from that of the Stoics or from the targums. (The similarity of John's usage to that of the Targum Neofiti has already been observed above.) For a summary of discussions on the issue, see Raymond Brown, *The Anchor Bible: The Gospel According to John* (Garden City, New York: Doubleday, 1966), pp. 519–524. In the opinion of the present writer any connection between the Stoic use of *logos* and that of John is more likely to have been due to the general diffusion of Hellenistic ideas throughout the eastern Mediterranean than to have been the result of direct borrowing.

13. *De Principiis* 4. 2. 2, in Jean Daniélou, *Origen* (New York: Sheed and Ward, 1955), p. 139.

ences of the central character Christian represent not those of a traveler in seventeenth century England, but those of the spiritual pilgrim in his journey to heaven. As a means of interpreting biblical texts, the allegorical method is characterized by the assumption that the author intended his work to be an allegory, and thus represents the search for the "spiritual" meaning of the text, for which its literal meaning is merely the vehicle.[14]

The Greeks used the allegorical method for positive and negative purposes. The positive purpose was to allow the ancient classics, which had come to have the status of canonical Scripture, to be interpreted to reflect then-modern philosophic and scientific opinion. In Book XV of Homer's Iliad, the high god Zeus warns the goddess Hera against continuing to interfere in the Trojan War:

> Nay, but yet I know not whether thou mayst not be the first to reap the fruits of thy cruel treason, and I beat thee with stripes, Dost thou not remember, when thou wert hung from on high, and from thy feet I suspended two anvils, and round thy hands fastened a golden bond that might not be broken? And thou didst hang in the clear air and the clouds, and the gods were wroth in high Olympus, but they could not come round and unloose thee.[15]

For Origen's opponent Celsus, however, the point of Zeus' speech to Hera is not mythological but cosmological:

> The words of Zeus to Hera are the words of God to matter.... The words to matter vaguely hint that at the beginning it was in

---

14. Some scholars prefer to use the term "typology" instead of "allegory" for the hermeneutic advocated by Origen. When this distinction is made, it is in the interest of differentiating an interpretation which recognizes the significance of the literal meaning of the text while also seeking its symbolic sense, from that which dismisses the literal meaning as insignificant and directs its full attention to the symbolic senses of the passage. The former is called "typology," the latter "allegory." "Allegory" is the term used by Origen for his method, and will be used in the present work to denote a broad approach to interpretation within which one's evaluation of the literal meaning may vary.

15. Andrew Lang, Walter Leaf, and Ernest Myers, *The Iliad of Homer* (New York: The Modern Library, n.d.), p. 266.

chaos and God divided it in certain proportions, bound it together, and ordered it.[16]

The literal meaning of Homer has become reinterpreted allegorically, so that the high god Zeus becomes the one God of Platonism, Hera becomes matter, and the act of punishment becomes the act of creation.

The negative purpose to which the allegorical method was put was to explain passages which, when they were taken at face value, seemed to lead to moral or theological error. The first-century Jewish philosopher Philo, who lived in the Hellenistic city of Alexandria, commonly used the allegorical method in interpreting of the Old Testament. An example is his treatment of Genesis 4:15–16, which reads:

> And the Lord put a mark on Cain, lest any who came upon him should kill him. Then Cain went out from the face of the Lord, and dwelt in the land of Nod, east of Eden.[17]

This passage presents a theological difficulty to Philo, who writes:

> Let us here raise the question whether in the books in which Moses acts as God's interpreter we ought to take his statements figuratively, since the impression made by the words in their literal sense is greatly at variance with truth.... For a face is a piece of a living creature, and God is a whole and not a part, so that we shall have to assign him the other parts of the body as well.... And if God has human forms and parts, he must needs also have human passions and experiences.[18]

For Philo there seems to be no end to the trouble which a literal reading of the text will bring: If God has a face, he must have the rest of the

16. Origen, *Contra Celsum,* ed. by Henry Chadwick (Cambridge: University Press, 1965), pp. 358–359.

17. This quotation follows the Revised Standard Version except for reading "from the face of" in place of "from the presence of," in order to preserve the feature on which Philo is commenting.

18. *De Posteritate Caini,* in C. K. Barrett, ed., *The New Testament Background* (New York: Harper and Row, 1961), p. 180.

body; and if he has a body, he must also have the passions and other problems which physical existence brings.

All that is left for Philo is to allegorize. An example of his use of the allegorical method is his discussion of the meaning of the two cherubim which, according to Exodus 25:20, were among the furnishings of the ancient Hebrew tabernacle.[19] This passage reads:

> The cherubim shall spread out their wings above, overshadowing the mercy seat with their wings, their faces one to another; toward the mercy seat shall the faces of the cherubim be.

Philo believed his interpretation of this passage to have been inspired by God:

> I have also, on one occasion, heard a more ingenious train of reasoning from my soul, which was accustomed frequently to be seized with a certain divine inspiration. . . . It told me that in the one living and true God there were two supreme and primary powers—goodness and authority; and that by his goodness he had created every thing, and by his authority he governed all that he had created; and that the third thing which was between the two, and had the effect of bringing them together, was reason, for it was owing to reason that God was both a ruler and good.[20]

By allegorizing, Philo finds a contemporary theological meaning in a passage which otherwise would have only been about ancient liturgical furniture, and only of historical importance.

The allegorical interpretation of the Bible entered the Christian

---

19. "Cherubim" is the plural, both in Hebrew and in English, of "cherub." (The construction "cherubims" is therefore incorrect, since "cherubim" is already plural.) Cherubim were winged figures, which may have resembled the sphinx-like figures which have been depicted in the religious art of the Near East. It is clear that the cherubim of Exodus 25 do not resemble the winged infants thought of as cherubs today.

20. *De Cherubin,* in Nahum N. Glatzer, ed., *The Essential Philo* (New York: Schocken Books, 1971), p. 78.

Church when Greek-educated people became Christians. In Galatians 4:21–26 Paul constructed an allegorical interpretation of the narrative of the births of Abraham's sons found in Genesis 16–17 and 21. The important features of this narrative, which is too long to reproduce here, are the following: Abraham, who had been promised an heir by God, has been urged by his wife Sarah to impregnate her maid Hagar, since Sarah is beyond the childbearing age and is thought to be sterile.[21] As a result of this act, a son named Ishmael is born, and later Sarah herself becomes pregnant and gives birth to Isaac. It is Isaac who is the heir whom God promised, as Genesis 21:12 states: "Through Isaac shall your descendants be named." For Paul, however, the significance of the narrative is not its literal meaning about the offspring of the patriarch, but its allegorical application to the issue in which Paul was embroiled: whether non-Jewish Christians are obligated to observe the Jewish Law. He writes:

> Tell me, you who desire to be under law, do you not hear the law? For it is written that Abraham had two sons, one by a slave and one by a free woman. But the son of the slave was born according to the flesh, the son of the free woman through promise. Now this is an allegory: these women are two covenants. One is from Mount Sinai, bearing children for slavery; she is Hagar. Now Hagar is Mount Sinai in Arabia; she corresponds to the present Jerusalem, for she is in slavery with her children. But the Jerusalem above is free, and she is our mother.

Once Paul begins to interpret the Genesis text allegorically, his conclusion is clear: Hagar is the convenant made at Mount Sinai; those who belong to that covenant are slaves in the same way Hagar was. Sarah is the new covenant made in Christ; those who belong to this covenant are

---

21. This practice, which seems morally peculiar to us, may have been required by law in the time of the patriarchs. According to the seventeenth-century B.C. Code of Hammurabi, the failure of a sterile wife to do as Sarah did is grounds for her husband to take a second wife. It was common in the ancient world to believe that the problem of a childless couple could only be on the part of the wife. This mistaken view is occasionally heard today.

free. The Jewish Law is part of the trappings of the old covenant and has no place in the lives of those who are free.

As Christianity became a separate religious movement from Judaism, the allegorical method increasingly became the Church's standard method of biblical interpretation. Since, as 2 Timothy 3:16 had said, *all* Scripture was thought to be profitable for teaching, Christians believed that Christian doctrine was to be found in the Old Testament as well as in the New. This doctrine was the spiritual truth of the Hebrew Scriptures and was hidden behind the literal meaning of the texts. The use of the allegorical method to uncover Christian truth was thought to have been authorized by Paul, who wrote in 2 Corinthians 3:6:

> [God] also hath made us able ministers of the new testament; not of the letter, but of the spirit; for the letter killeth, but the spirit giveth life.[22]

An example of the use of the allegorical method to extract Christian doctrine from the Old Testament is found in Augustine's *The City of God,* written during the early fifth century. In Genesis 6:15–16, which Augustine interprets, Noah is given instructions how to build the ark:

> This is how you are to make it: the length of the ark three hundred cubits, its breadth fifty cubits, and its height thirty cubits.[23] Make a roof for the ark, and finish it to a cubit above; and set the door of the ark in its side; make it with lower, second, and third decks.

---

22. King James Version. Paul's intended distinction is not between literal and spiritual hermeneutics but between living by the law and living by the Spirit. The Revised Standard Version, together with other modern translations, preserves Paul's intention by rendering the last part of the verse: "... not in a written code but in the Spirit; for the written code kills, but the Spirit gives life."

23. A cubit was a unit of measurement of about eighteen to twenty inches. Initially a cubit was measured by one's forearm from the elbow to the tip of the longest fingers; a standard cubit may have been used in later building projects.

Augustine interprets this passage as an allegory of Christ.[24]

> Without doubt this is a symbol of the City of God on pilgrimage
> in this world, of the Church which is saved through the wood on
> which was suspended "the mediator between God and men, the
> man Christ Jesus." The actual measurements of the ark, its
> length, height, and breadth, symbolize the human body, in the
> reality of which Christ was to come, and did come, to mankind.
> For the length of the human body from the top of its head to the
> sole of its foot is six times its breadth and ten times its depth,
> measured from back to belly.... That is why the ark was made
> 300 cubits in length, fifty cubits in breadth, and thirty in height.
> And the door which it was given in its side surely represents the
> wound made when the side of the crucified was pierced with
> the spear. This, as we know, is the way of entrance for those
> who come to him, because from that wound flowed the sacra-
> ments with which believers are initiated.[25]

Everything in the narrative is allegorized. The ark is the church, the
wood is the cross, the dimensions are those of a man, and the door is the
wound in the side of Jesus.

In addition to the application of the allegorical method as a means
of reading the Old Testament as a textbook in Christian theology, there
were other, less clearly articulated reasons which contributed to its use
in the Church. One of these was the prevailing philosophical mood. The
philosophy of Neo-Platonism taught that this world is the lowest of
several stages of emanation from God, of which our universe is the
farthest removed from its Source. As a result, the things in this world
are only "frivolities, nothing but phantoms in a phantom, like something in a mirror which really exists in one place but is reflected in
another. It seems to be filled but holds nothing; it is all seeming."[26] A

---

24. Augustine acknowledges the literal meaning of the text elsewhere and argues that
the flood account is historically possible, in *City of God* XV, 27, Henry Bettenson, trans.
(Baltimore: Penguin Books, 1972), pp. 645–648.

25. *Ibid.*, XV, 26, pp. 643–644.

26. *Enneads*, III, 6, 7, quoted by George F. Thomas, *Religious Philosophies of the West*
(New York: Charles Scribner's Sons, 1965), p. 57.

related metaphor had earlier been used by Plato: we are like prisoners in a cave who can only see the back wall of the cave, against which are projected the shadows of those who pass behind the prisoners between them and the light. We, the prisoners, see the shadows and mistakenly take them to be the realities. The influence of Neo-Platonism was pervasive and not limited to those who had read Plato. An effect of this philosophy on Christianity was to emphasize the otherworldly and the spiritual at the expense of the present world and its affairs. In the area of Christian piety, this added encouragement to monasticism and mysticism. In the area of biblical interpretation, it furthered the search for the spiritual meaning of the Bible, which was considered to be beyond its literal sense.

An additional factor which encouraged the use of the allegorical method was its usefulness in theological controversy. On the one hand, the use of this method allowed the interpreter to locate a large number of biblical passages in support of his position. We have seen an example of this above when Paul interprets allegorically to support his rejection of the Mosaic law. Perhaps an equally important use in debates, however, was that the allegorical method allowed one to explain passages which, if taken literally, might undermine one's own position. There exists a report on a conversation between Origen and two heretics who denied the immortality of the soul on the grounds of Leviticus 17:11. The latter passage reads, "For the life of the flesh is in the blood. . . ." If, they reasoned, life is in the blood, it follows that one cannot survive the death of the body. A contemporary reader might have expected Origen to distinguish between physical and spiritual survival. Instead, we are told that he allegorizes:

> Origen collects many texts where the bodily members and the five senses are employed in a figurative sense. Sometimes, in explaining the figure, he finds a deeper meaning. Thus *the very hairs of your head are all numbered* was said to the disciples who were Nazarenes with shaven heads, and hence it must refer to spiritual protection. It follows that the blood which is mentioned in these two texts of the Law must belong to the interior man, as we read in Genesis: *of the blood of your souls*

account will be asked. So the prohibition to eat flesh which has the lifeblood in it does not refer to the blood of the body.[27]

By finding a deeper meaning in Leviticus 17:11, Origen has deflected the point of his opponents' use of this passage.

As the allegorical method came to be the Church's standard tool for interpreting the Bible, its use became increasingly complex. Paul can find two meanings in a passage: its literal, historical sense, and its allegorical, spiritual interpretation. Although his application of a passage might be ethical (as in 1 Corinthians 9:9–10) or theological (as in Galatians 4:21–26), no systematic attempt was made to distinguish between different levels of allegorical meaning. Such a distinction was made by Origen who, on the basis of the terms "spirit, soul, and body" in 1 Thessalonians 5:23, differentiated between the bodily or literal sense, the soul or the moral sense, and the spiritual or the mystical sense of a text. The multiplication of meanings was completed by the Middle Ages, by which time every passage was thought to have four meanings. These were the literal or historical, the allegorical or doctrinal, the moral or ethical, and the anagogical or heavenly. A classic example is the then-standard fourfold interpretation of the word "Jerusalem" in Galatians 4:26, "But the Jerusalem above is free, and she is our mother." Literally, "Jerusalem" means the ancient city; allegorically, it means the Church of Christ; morally, it means the soul; anagogically, it means the heavenly city. The fourfold allegorical interpretation of the Bible was commonly used throughout the Middle Ages. Its great attractiveness was that it allowed any passage of the Bible to be used in the work of the theologians and in the instruction of the people in their faith.

The allegorical method is a systematic reinterpretation of the literal details of a passage in the interest of its usefulness to the contemporary commentator. The concern of the allegorical interpreter is similar to those of the targumist or the typologist. The allegorical method differs from these methods, however, in that it distinguishes between a passage's literal and applied senses, and acknowledges that the fuller

---

27. Beryl Smalley, *The Study of the Bible in the Middle Ages* (Notre Dame, Indiana: University of Notre Dame Press, 1964), p. 57.

meanings may not have been in the mind of the original author. As we shall see in the following section, the rise of the literal method began to limit the more imaginative uses of an allegorical interpretation. Most modern biblical scholars distinguish carefully between the meaning of a passage for its author and original readers, and the application of that meaning to modern issues of faith and life.

The Literal Method. Although the allegorical method had become the standard Christian tool for interpreting the Bible during the Middle Ages, it was not without its critics. One of the objections to the method concerned the number of meanings a passage might be thought to have: if any number of interpretations could be found in a passage, how is the Christian to know when he or she has understood the text correctly? This objection was anticipated by Augustine, who, as we have seen, used the method:

> When so many meanings, all of them acceptable as true, can be extracted from the words that Moses wrote, do you not see how foolish it is to make a bold assertion that one in particular is the one he had in mind? Do you not see how foolish it is to enter into mischievous arguments which are an offense against that very charity for the sake of which he wrote every one of the words that we are trying to explain?[28]

If the fact of multiple interpretations indicated to Augustine a need for Christian charity, it indicated to its critics a need for methodological precision.

The objection of the literal interpreters to the allegorizers was that, by finding symbols everywhere in the Bible, the latter failed to distinguish between those passages which were designated as symbolic and those which were not so designated and were thus to be understood literally. St. John Chrysostom, an advocate of literal interpretation, noted, "Everywhere in Scripture there is this law, that when it allego-

---

28. *Confessions* XII, 25, R. S. Pine-Coffin, trans. (Baltimore: Penguin Books, 1961), p. 303.

rizes, it also gives the explanation of the allegory."[29] The literal method asserts that the words of the Bible are to be understood normally, in the same senses that these words would have in a non-biblical context. The key to understanding a passage is the intention of its author, and this is discovered by observing the textual and historical context in which the passage is found. A sixth-century manual of biblical interpretation, Junilius Africanus' *Institutes of the Divine Law,* stated:

> What should we keep in mind for the understanding of the scriptures? What is said must be suited to him who says it, it must not disagree with the causes for which it is said, and it must agree with the times, places, order of events, and intention of scripture.[30]

Theodore of Mopsuestia in the fifth century opposed the common hermeneutic practice of finding references to Jesus throughout the Old Testament. He wrote that the Old Testament was written for the primary advantage of its original readers, and refused to grant a christological meaning to more than four psalms or to the Song of Solomon.

The use of the term "literal" to denote this method does not imply that its practitioners were forced to overlook figures of speech in the Bible or to ignore those Old Testament passages which are identified in the New Testament as having been fulfilled in the career of Jesus. With regard to the former, the literal interpreters simply asserted that words are to be understood normally. Normal usage includes figures of speech, and when Robert E. Lee called General Thomas J. Jackson "Stonewall," his hearers did not assume that Lee thought Jackson was constructed of granite. Similarly, to recognize the metaphor in Jesus' statement, "I am the door" (John 10:9), does not violate the principle of literal interpretation. With regard to the latter, the literalists believed that Old Testament writers were sometimes given prophetic insight into the future so that things they said or did were actual prophecies about Jesus. They

---

29. *Commentary on Isaiah,* quoted by Robert M. Grant, *A Short History of the Interpretation of the Bible* (New York: Macmillan, 1963), p. 103.

30. Quoted by Grant, *History,* p. 100.

insisted, however, that the prophetic quality of such passages was inherent in their authors' intention and was not the product of later allegorical interpretation.

Two centers of literally-oriented biblical study were Antioch during the fifth and sixth centuries and Paris in the eleventh and twelfth centuries. Among the scholars of Antioch were St. John Chrysostom and Theodore of Mopsuestia, whose views we have already observed. Among those of Paris were the friars Hugh and Andrew of the Abbey of St. Victor. Hugh wrote that any interpretation of a passage must begin with its literal sense:

> I wonder how people have the face to boast themselves teachers of allegory, when they do not know the primary meaning of the letter. "We read the Scriptures," they say, "but we don't read the letter. The letter does not interest us. We teach allegory." How do you read Scripture then, if you don't read the letter? Subtract the letter and what is left? ... Do not despise what is lowly in God's word, for by lowliness you will be enlightened to divinity. The outward form of God's word seems to you, perhaps, like dirt, so you trample it underfoot, like dirt, and despise what the letter tells you physically and visibly. But hear! that dirt, which you trample, opened the eyes of the blind.[31]

Both at Antioch and at Paris, the origin of Christian literal interpretation was in rabbinic exegetical midrash. Robert M. Grant has written concerning Antioch:

> For centuries the Jewish community there was prominent and influential. The earliest Antiochene exegesis which we possess, an interpretation of Genesis of Theophilus of Antioch, is largely derived from Jewish teachers. ... A little later we find Dortheus, head of the catechetical school of Antioch, studying Hebrew. And some of the interpretations of Theodore of Mopsuestia are

---

31. *De Scripturis* V. 13–15, quoted by Smalley, *The Bible in the Middle Ages,* pp. 93–94.

criticized by his disciple Theodoret as being Jewish rather than Christian. Naturally these interpreters rejected allegorization.[32]

In a similar way, the friars of St. Victor were influenced by the rabbis with whom they studied the Old Testament. Hugh wrote:

> We have set forth the explanation of this book, as far as the gist is concerned, for the greater part without any alteration, according to others, who like ourselves have been instructed on the literal sense of the Pentateuch by the Jews.[33]

It was by means of this contract that they were introduced to the Jewish literal hermeneutic tradition which was used by Rashi and other medieval Jewish scholars. As was the case in Antioch, contact with the rabbinic tradition renewed interest among Christians in the literal method of interpreting of the Bible.

If the source of the literal method was rabbinic exegesis, the occasion of its revitalization in the Church was a shift in the philosophic base of Christian scholarship. We have seen that the philosophy of Neo-Platonism encouraged the search for the spiritual sense behind the merely literal meaning of the Bible. By the thirteenth century, the philosophy of Aristotle had begun to replace Neo-Platonism as the intellectual framework for Christian thought. An essential difference between Aristotle and the Neo-Platonists had to do with the nature of reality. We have seen that for the Neo-Platonists, the world of perception was thought to be merely the reflection of a higher ultimate reality. For Aristotle the opposite was the case. What exist are concrete, individual substances; what Neo-Platonism thought to be transcendent realities are to Aristotle merely abstractions which depend on concrete phenomena for their existence. An effect of the Aristotelian emphasis on the concrete in place of the abstract was the discovery that the concrete literal sense was to be the basis for all other interpretations of the Bible. St. Thomas Aquinas, who employed Aristotelianism in the

---

32. *History*, pp. 89–90.
33. Quoted by Smalley, *The Bible in the Middle Ages*, p. 127.

service of Christian theology in his monumental *Summa Theologiae,* wrote:

> Now because the literal sense is that which the author intends, and the author of Holy Scripture is God who comprehends everything all at once in his understanding, it comes not amiss, as St. Augustine observes, if many meanings are present even in the literal sense of one passage of Scripture.... Consequently holy Scripture sets up no confusion, since all meanings are based on one, namely the literal sense. From this alone can arguments be drawn, and not, as St. Augustine remarks in his letter to Vincent the Donatist, from the things said by allegory. Nor does this undo the effect of holy Scripture, for nothing necessary for the faith is contained under the spiritual sense that is not openly conveyed through the literal sense elsewhere.[34]

Whereas the literal sense of the Bible became the primary sense for later Catholic interpreters, Protestant scholars tended to make it the only allowable interpretation. Martin Luther deviated from an exclusively literal hermeneutic only in stating that, in addition to its literal sense, "every word in the Bible points to Christ."[35] John Calvin rejected all non-literal interpretations of the Bible, and, in the words of John T. McNeill, "cites Scripture only as authenticating what it directly says."[36] The high point of literal interpretation was perhaps seventeenth-century Protestantism. Particularly in the Calvinistic tradition, the literal method was combined with logical analysis to produce a theological system which was the Protestant equivalent of Thomas Aquinas' *Summa Theologiae.* The hermeneutical principles of this system were explicitly stated in the Westminster Confession of Faith:

---

34. *Summa Theologiae* Ia, 1, 10, Thomas Cilby, trans. (New York: McGraw-Hill, 1964), Vol. 1, p. 39.

35. Martin Luther, *Lectures on Romans,* Wilhelm Rauck, trans. (Philadelphia: Westminster, 1961), p. 288.

36. John Calvin, *Institutes of the Christian Religion,* Ford Lewis Battles, trans. (Philadelphia: Westminster, 1960), Vol. 1, p. liv.

The whole counsel of God, concerning all things necessary for his own glory, man's salvation, faith, and life, is either expressly set down in Scripture, or by good and necessary consequence may be deduced from Scripture, unto which nothing at any time is to be added. . . . All things in Scripture are not alike plain in themselves, nor alike clear unto all; yet those things which are necessary to be known, believed, and observed, for salvation, are so clearly propounded and opened in some place of Scripture or other, that not only the learned, but the unlearned, in a due use of the ordinary means, may attain unto a sufficient understanding of them. . . . The infallible rule of interpretation of Scripture is the Scripture itself; and therefore, when there is a question about the true and full sense of any Scripture (which is not manifold, but one), it must be searched and known by other places that speak more clearly.[37]

Both Catholics and Protestants believed that an authoritative guide to Christian faith and living was necessary. Whereas Catholics found this guide in the Church, Protestants found it in the Bible, which they believed to be self-interpreting and, under the guidance of the Spirit, sufficiently clear even to the theologically untrained.[38]

The literal method of biblical interpretation is based on the meaning intended by the author himself, and seeks to understand these words in much the same way as one would interpret any other written text. Words are understood in their literary contexts and as conveying their normal meanings. Although this method came to be used by Protestants in the defense of positions already arrived at on theological grounds, the literal method became the normative way by which Protestants understood the Bible. It was used in Catholicism as a way of checking the

---

37. I, 6–9, in John H. Leith, *Creeds of the Churches* (Garden City, New York: Doubleday Anchor, 1963), pp. 195–196.

38. As we have seen in Chapter 1, the issues of the authority and the interpretation of the Bible were especially important to Protestants. The Protestant concept that the Bible is adequately self-explaining is called the "doctrine of the perspicuity of the Scripture," and was formulated as a counter to the Catholic view that the Church is the divinely-commissioned interpreter of the Bible.

uncontrolled allegorizing which typified earlier medieval biblical study. Refined by the application of the insights and tools of modern biblical scholarship, the literal method continues to be used by contemporary theologians.

It should not be concluded from the preceding discussion, however, that a responsible use of something like an allegorical approach to the Bible ceased with the development of the literal method. Although, as we shall see below, an historically-informed version of the literal method has become the primary tool of most contemporary biblical scholars, a carefully limited use of allegory which is sometimes known as "typology" continues to be of use to many modern theologians and devotional readers of the Bible. The term "typology" comes from the Greek word *typos,* which may mean a model, an example, or a pattern. The principle employed in a typological reading of the Bible is the recognition that many references, especially in the Old Testament, may serve the Christian reader as reminders and illustrations of important New Testament concepts which are not actually taught in the passage being read.

When, for instance, the Christian reader of the Genesis account of the flood thinks as he or she reads, "Yes! Just as they were preserved from harm by an ark which God provided, we are saved in an even greater way by the work of Christ," he or she is thinking of the ark as a "type" of Christ. The difference between a typological understanding of the flood narrative and the classical allegorical explanation which was employed by Augustine is that the typological interpreter recognizes that his insight is his own, and not the point intended by the passage's original author. That the Christian reader of Genesis 6 is reminded of the salvation which Christians believe comes through Christ is altogether an appropriate response to the passage; what is less appropriate, by contemporary standards of biblical interpretation, is the occasionally-made assumption that such a reference to Christ was the intention of the passage's author. Such an assumption, although devotionally satisfying, may actually prevent the reader from exploring what the writer himself intended to say.

To interpret a passage typologically is to be reminded of Christian doctrines which may be taught elsewhere in the Bible, and to apply these concepts in one's devotional or theological reflection, without concluding that these ideas are necessarily the point of the passage at hand. This limited application of the allegorical method will continue to be useful to the devotional reader of the Bible. One who is primarily interested in studying the Bible itself, who of course may on other occasions also be a devotional reader, will be better served not by the typological method, but by the historical modifications to the literal method which will be described below.

Interpreting the Bible Today

The greatest weakness in the application of the older methods of biblical interpretation was that their practitioners tended to ignore the immense historical and cultural gap between the Bible and the modern reader, and so, for example, if they lived in England during the seventeenth century, they were inclined to read the Bible as though it had been written by seventeenth century Englishmen. By contrast, that which distinguishes contemporary ways of interpreting the Bible from those employed earlier is above all the historical awareness of the modern interpreter. The contemporary scholar is consciously aware of the gap which separates himself from the times and culture of the biblical writers, and does not assume that the Bible was written in his own linguistic or cultural idiom. Thus, as the development of the modern discipline of historical science helped biblical scholars to become aware of the distance between themselves and the Bible's first readers, the literal method came to be supplemented by historical techniques of biblical study. The tools most commonly associated with this effort were originally forged during the nineteenth century with the development of what is known as the historical-critical method.[39]

The Historical-Critical Method. Although its antecedents may be traced earlier, the development of an historical approach to the Bible occurred primarily during the nineteenth century. Robert M. Grant has observed that the new approach to biblical studies was itself the result of a change in the setting in which the study of the Bible took place. As a

---

39. It will be recalled that "critical" means "intellectually careful," and need not imply a destructive attitude or outcome.

result of the special relationship between Church and state in Germany, the training of the clergy took place not in academically isolated theological schools but in the state universities. This brought the study of the Bible, which previously had been under the control of religious authorities, into the sphere of influence of secular methods of academic research.[40] Among the methods which came to be applied to the Bible was the new scientific approach to history, which had been used with great success in the investigation of other aspects of the ancient past.

The fruitfulness of this approach to the study of the past may be illustrated by Heinrich Schliemann's discovery of the site of ancient Troy in 1870. Prior to the work of Schliemann it had been customary to regard the writings of Homer as mythological poems with no basis in historical fact. Schliemann carefully compared topographical details in the ancient writings with actual sites on the coast of Asia Minor, and succeeded in identifying the location of the ancient city of Troy. Subsequent archaeological investigations uncovered arrowheads of a Greek type and revealed evidence that the city had been destroyed by Greek invaders, confirming the historical fact, if not the details, of the war described by Homer.[41]

Two important features of the new historical method may be observed in connection with the work of Schliemann. The first is that the old distinction between historical narratives on the one hand and fictional writings on the other was discarded in favor of a view which recognized that a given document might contain a mixture of legendary materials and genuine historical recollections. As Schliemann had demonstrated in the case of the Iliad, myth and history could be combined by an ancient writer and co-exist in the same writing. The second characteristic of the new historical discipline concerned the role of the historian. Instead of identifying documents from the past which were believed to be historically reliable, and then somewhat passively assembling their contents into a narrative, the new historian was actively to be the judge of the ancient records, separating fictional from historical elements, and conferring authority on those portions of the records which

---

40. Grant, *History,* pp. 153–154.
41. See J. V. Luce, *Homer and the Heroic Age* (New York: Harper and Row, 1975), pp. 15–18; M. I. Finley, *The World of Odysseus* (London: Chatto & Windus, 1964), pp. 45–46.

passed the test of his scientific scrutiny. The goal of the new historian was to tell the truth about the past in a way which the ancient narrators themselves could not, and to describe each event, in the words of Leopold von Ranke, *wie es eigentlich gewesen ist*—"the way it actually happened."[42]

It was initially feared by many that the new historical scholarship would prove destructive to the Christian faith, and several Christian groups reacted negatively to its use. Among those who rejected the new scholarship were the fundamentalists. The term "fundamentalist" was taken from the title of a series of theological works which were published between 1910 and 1915 under the sponsorship of a wealthy businessman named Lyman Stewart. *The Fundamentals,* as the twelve books were called, were intended to provide a rebuttal to the new liberal and critical thought. These volumes were mailed free to every theological professor, minister, and ministerial student in the United States. Although these works were not generally successful in persuading scholars and theologians to abandon an historical approach to the Bible, their theme of defending the doctrines which were thought to be fundamental to Christianity became the rallying point of a number of conservative movements within Protestantism.

The doctrines which *The Fundamentals* sought to defend were, in general, classical Christian concepts, such as the virgin birth of Jesus, his atoning death, and his physical resurrection. In defending these teachings, the fundamentalists adopted as a doctrine a more recent idea which they thought to be epistemologically necessary for the maintenance of the more traditional doctrines. This was their conception of the inspiration and the inerrancy of the Bible.

Christians had always believed that the Bible was God's revelation and was authoritative in matters of Christian faith and practice. The fundamentalists redefined this general statement as meaning that the Bible, as God's Word in written form, was totally without error both in its central teachings and in historical and scientific matters upon which it incidentally touched. This specific idea was not held by the Protestant

---

42. For a description of the new historical method and a discussion of its application and problems for biblical study, see Van A. Harvey, *The Historian and The Believer* (New York: Macmillan, 1966), especially Chapters 1–3.

reformers of the sixteenth century who generally recognized the possibility of human fallibility in the non-essential statements of the Bible. For instance, it did not trouble John Calvin that the author of Matthew 27:9 incorrectly cited Isaiah instead of Zechariah as the source of his Old Testament quotation. The idea that the biblical authors were in some way freed from all sorts of error was developed by later Protestant theologians, and provided Protestants with a theoretical basis for the correctness of their teachings in much the same way as did the doctrine of the infallibility of the Church for Roman Catholics.

The classical statement of the doctrine of biblical inerrancy was that of the Presbyterian theologian B. B. Warfield, who argued that the biblical authors were inspired in the same way as were the Old Testament prophets, so that the statement "it is written" means the same thing as the prophetic "thus says the Lord." Since, Warfield reasoned, God cannot lie, then his words in the Bible can contain nothing but the truth, whether in their essential teachings or in more secondary matters of science and history. This conception of the inerrancy of the Bible was applied by Warfield only to the original manuscripts of the Bible, but it was adopted somewhat less critically by the fundamentalists, who applied it to the King James Version of the Bible, and used it in defending not only the classical doctrines of Christianity but also such less traditional concepts as the idea that God created the world in six actual days in the spring of the year 4004 B.C. Increasingly, the fundamentalists came to rely on their view of the inerrancy of Scripture to resolve complex historical questions rather than to engage in scholarly research into the issues themselves.[43]

---

43. A recent development in conservative Protestant circles has been the rise of a movement which its adherents have sometimes called a "new evangelicalism." The leaders of this movement include biblical scholars and theologians who were raised as fundamentalists but who have come to reject the fundamentalist attitude of separation from non-fundamentalist believers and scholars. Evangelicals have typically been less dogmatic than the older fundamentalists on matters of the historical and scientific inerrancy of the Bible and of millennial theology, and have often demonstrated an acceptance of non-fundamentalists both as fellow believers and as academic colleagues. Many evangelical scholars have re-entered the academic discussions which their theological forefathers abandoned, and have often contributed to the study of the Bible, especially in matters of textual criticism.

As the fundamentalists found that their theologically-based conclusions failed to persuade historical scholars, they began to withdraw from the field of academic discussion and sometimes even separated themselves from other Christians with whom they did not theologically agree. Fundamentalism eventually came to be associated not only with biblical literalism and separatism but also with millennialism. Interest in the millennium had been an undercurrent in Christianity since the first century, and millennial ideas were held by some of the more radical Protestant reformers. Millennial doctrines were revived in England during the nineteenth century and were a major emphasis in the theology of a preacher of the Plymouth Brethren Church named John Darby. Darby taught that the second coming of Christ would occur in two stages. First, Christ would appear in the skies and would take Christian believers back with him into heaven. Seven years later, Christ would return to earth with the believers and inaugurate the kingdom of God. Since Darby's view was that the second coming would occur before the millennium, this doctrine has been called "pre-millennialism." Darby's doctrine, although never adopted by the majority of Protestant theologians, was incorporated into the notes of the *Scofield Reference Bible,* and is generally held by fundamentalists today.

In addition to the reactions of the fundamentalists, efforts were made in several larger denominations to limit the use of the historical-critical method by Christian biblical scholars. In the Roman Catholic Church, the Pontifical Biblical Commission was charged with ruling authoritatively on matters of biblical scholarship which concerned issues thought to be vital to Catholic theology. Some Protestant denominations subjected the practitioners of the new methods to charges of heresy. A series of heresy trials in the Presbyterian Church in the U.S.A. sought to impose a methodological orthodoxy on that denomination's theologians and biblical scholars.[44] Indeed, it seemed for a while that the fears about the new historical scholarship were well founded. Some of the new scholars were theological liberals whose religious opinions were more derived from the ideas of contemporary philosophers than

---

44. See Lefferts Loetscher's history of Presbyterian theological controversies: *The Broadening Church* (Philadelphia: University of Pennsylvania Press, 1954).

from the Bible. As the critics began to raise questions about the historical reliability of the Scriptures and the fundamentalists reacted against
the new methods and chose to remain isolated from academic research
and discussion, the immediate result seemed to be an isolation of historical study from Christian theology on both sides.

This, however, was not to be the case. While the more radical critics
were startling the world of biblical scholarship by their research, more
moderate practitioners of the historical-critical method had begun to
correct many of the radicals' theories. In response to F. C. Baur's Hegeli-
an reconstruction of early Christian history,[45] J. B. Lightfoot recon-
firmed the antiquity of the earliest Christian writings. In response to the
assertion of critics that the patriarchal accounts in Genesis were retro-
jected legends and customs of the later Hebrews, biblical archaeologists
and historians demonstrated the compatibility of the narratives with
what is known of Middle Bronze Age culture in Palestine.[46] In short, the
historical-critical method proved to be less destructive than its early
opponents had feared. The contributions of historical studies have come
to be seen by most scholars as far outweighing the problems which
seemed to emerge when the new methods were first applied to the study
of the Bible.

To read a portion of the Bible is in many ways like reading someone
else's mail (this is literally the case in the New Testament, much of
which consists of letters). To avoid misunderstanding, the contemporary reader needs to have information about its author, its occasion, and
its readers—all of which did not need to be told to its original recipients,
and is usually omitted from the text itself. The various tools of historical
study have provided much of this and other information to the modern
interpreter. The discipline known as textual criticism (described in
Chapter 3 above) has enabled scholars to recover with a high degree

---

45. Baur had applied Hegel's view of history to Christianity, and argued that an
original Jewish Christianity was opposed by the Gentile Christianity of Paul, and that the
tension between these was finally resolved in the synthesis he called "proto-Catholicism."
See Stephen Neill, *The Interpretation of the New Testament, 1861–1961* (Oxford: Oxford
University Press, 1966), pp. 19–25, 53–56.

46. See W. F. Albright, "The Old Testament and the Archaeology of Palestine," in H.
H. Rowley, ed., *The Old Testament and Modern Study* (Oxford: Oxford University Press,
1961), pp. 1–7.

of assurance what the authors originally wrote. Source criticism has clarified the relationships among the historical writings of the Old Testament and among the Christian Gospels and has allowed us to understand some of the sources used in the composition of these writings. Form criticism has shed light on how the biblical materials were remembered and used before they were put into writing. Redaction criticism has investigated the ways the authors employed and arranged their materials in order to communicate their convictions.[47] (The contributions of these disciplines underscore the fact that the term "criticism" refers to careful methods of procedure, and need not imply a destructive attitude or outcome.) The results which have been obtained from the use of these tools have been incorporated in notes supplied in study editions of the Bible, and are described in many of the resource books described in the following chapter.

As a result of the contributions of historical scholarship to the study of the Bible, we are far better prepared than were previous generations of interpreters to bridge the centuries separating us from the writers of the Bible and to understand just what it was that they believed and sought to communicate to their first readers. One of the important by-products of the historical approach to biblical study has been to allow modern scholars to focus their attention on the text itself, and so to go behind the denominational controversies that were often characteristic of earlier periods of biblical study. This spirit has led to a higher degree of objectivity in the interpretation of the Bible, and has permitted the sort of ecumenical cooperation in biblical scholarship which has been observed in the preceding chapters of the present book.

Reading the Bible for Faith and Living. Many of the readers of the present book may be interested in reading the Bible as a guide to their own theological thinking and daily living, so it may be appropriate to conclude this chapter with some remarks about how such a person may

---

47. A detailed description of these methods is beyond the scope of an introductory book. The reader interested in pursuing these matters further may wish to consult the appropriate articles in the *Interpreter's Dictionary of the Bible* or the Guides to Biblical Scholarship series of small books published by Fortress Press. An excellent introduction to form criticism for the non-specialist, and a good way of observing modern biblical scholarship at work, is Gerhard Lohfink's *The Bible: Now I Get It!* (Garden City, N.Y.: Doubleday, 1979).

approach the Bible. (The reader who is interested in the Bible more as a literary or historical document than as a religious resource may wish to skip to the next chapter and rejoin us there.)

The limitations which are necessarily involved in the suggestions which follow must be clearly understood. The first is that what follows is intended to be only a beginning introduction to ways by which the Christian reader may begin to read the Bible profitably; it is in no way intended to be a complete discussion of the art and science of biblical interpretation. The writer is fully aware of the limitations in attempting to make a few suggestions for the use of the Bible in only a few pages. A second limitation concerns the skills which the non-specialized reader may be expected to have. The professional interpreter of the Bible must be able to consult its text in its original languages; it is assumed that the reader of this book cannot. The biblical scholar is expected to have grounded himself thoroughly in the history and the cultures of the Bible; this is not expected of the reader of this book. Yet one must start somewhere. The purpose of what follows, like an appetizer, is to whet the appetite, not to provide the full meal. It is important that the reader who works through these suggestions not conclude that this is all that one might need to know in order to become a qualified interpreter of the Bible.

1. A beginning point in the interpretation of a biblical passage is to discover its literal meaning. A devotional reader of Scripture may see in a particular passage a reminder of a truth which is explicitly taught elsewhere in the Bible but which is not the point of the text at hand. The latter is often the case when those who read the Bible as part of their daily devotional discipline seek a "daily blessing" as a sort of Christian motto for the day. These ways of reading the Bible may continue to be of value for devotional or perhaps even for homiletical purposes. They should not, however, become the primary method of the beginning interpreter. The common conviction of Christians has been that God's Word is in some way heard among the words of the people who wrote the Scriptures. An insistence on a literal interpretation as a first step in understanding the Bible is to assure that what is heard is this divine communication and not just the creative imagination of the interpreter.

2. The interpretation of a biblical text should be controlled by its

immediate context. Not all passages in the Bible deal with the main-stream of biblical theology, and one is well-advised not to force a theological perspective on a passage when that was not intended by its author. This principle is also the most effective check on the fact expressed by the truism, "You can prove anything by the Bible." One can even "prove" that "there is no God," by quoting from Psalm 14:1 or its parallel, Psalm 53:1. This can be done, however, only by ignoring the preceding clause, "the fool says in his heart. . . ." Most of the time, of course, one's ignoring of the context of a passage of the Bible is not so obvious as in this instance. The reason why citing biblical texts in support of one's convictions has gotten a bad reputation as "proof-texting" is that those making such citations have often lifted words from their contexts, applied them in support of ideas foreign to the thought of their writers, and used them in ways which can be seen to be inappropriate, by a reading of the context from which they were taken. One cannot prove, as the author once attempted, the Calvinistic doctrine that Christians cannot lose their salvation by quoting Ecclesiastes 3:14: "I know that whatever God does endures for ever." The author is talking about God's purposes for the created order, and surely not about any doctrine of salvation. Ignoring the context of a passage—including its immediate surroundings, the chapter(s) in which it is found, and the book in which it appears (and perhaps even the thought of its author as found throughout his writings)—will usually result in distorting the meaning of the text. It is a useful and succinct reminder that "a text without its context is only a pretext."[48]

The context of a passage, however, is not only its literary surroundings but also its historical and cultural setting. It is here that the contributions of historical scholarship have their greatest importance for the reader of the Bible. To repeat an earlier remark, to read the Bible is like reading a letter addressed to someone else: information about its writer, its occasion, and its first readers is often necessary for its correct interpretation. The understanding of any passage in the Bible will be

---

48. Quoted by A. Berkeley Mickelsen, *Interpreting the Bible* (Grand Rapids, Michigan: Eerdmans, 1963), p. 113. Mickelsen's book is a textbook in the exegesis of biblical passages. Its emphasis is more on literary than historical matters, and it is oriented around a Protestant evangelicalism.

aided by a knowledge of its cultural and historical setting, and for many passages an understanding of this sort of background is essential. Isaiah 7:14, which is often read as though the prophet's main point was to predict the birth of Jesus, requires a knowledge of the international situation facing the kingdom of Judah in the eighth century B.C.[49] Jesus' injunction in Matthew 4:41 that one should go two miles with the person who compels him to go one presumes that the reader knows of the law which allowed civilians to be ordered to assist in transporting government baggage. No interpretation of the Book of Revelation can be considered responsible which is ignorant of the persecution of Christians under the reign of Domitian, and of the way symbols were commonly used in Jewish apocalyptic writings. Many of the resources described in the following chapter are useful to provide these kinds of information.

3. A careful distinction should be made between the intended meaning of the passage in its own context and the reader's application of it to his or her own situation. Left to itself, an historical approach to the Bible might be thought to isolate the Scripture in the ancient past, with little value for the life of its modern reader. That which distinguishes the Christian reader of the Bible from the historian (who, of course, may also be a Christian) is that the former seeks to find in his reading something for his own theological, ethical, or devotional use. Especially for the beginning interpreter, there is the danger that one's present-day application may be confused with what the author actually wrote in his own time. Many of the difficulties associated with earlier methods of biblical interpretation were caused by a violation of this principle. The writer's point is always expressed in terms of the culture of his own time (indeed, it could not have been otherwise, if his writing were to have been understood). For the passage's first readers, its original meaning and its value for their lives were identical. For the modern reader whose cultural setting is different from that of the author, it is necessary to establish some sort of bridge between the historical significance of the text and its present-day application. One way by which this

---

49. Matthew's application of this passage to Jesus in 1:23 is a product of his conviction that, even more than the child to be born in the reign of Ahaz, Jesus is truly Immanuel, "God-is-with-us."

may be done is to identify the principle underlying the writer's words, and then—somewhat like extrapolation—to apply that principle to one's situation today.

An example of how we may apply a text to life today may be seen in connection with Galatians 3:28, which reads:

> There is neither Jew nor Greek, there is neither slave nor free, there is neither male nor female; for you are all one in Christ Jesus.

Paul is here talking about relationships within the Christian community. Even though prejudice existed in the larger Roman society, this was not to be the case among Christians. His principle is clearly stated: "for you are all one in Christ Jesus." A common sort of discrimination today is racial prejudice, but Paul does not mention this in Galatians 3:28. May we conclude from his silence that distinctions based on race are permissible to Christians (as did some whites in an earlier generation)? This conclusion is forbidden when one properly applies Paul's principle. Even though he does not mention racism (this was not a major problem in the Roman Empire; people were discriminated against on other grounds),[50] Paul's principle is clear: in Christ we are all one. The application to the present situation is made by identifying the principle applied by Paul in the first century in order to discover what this principle would have demanded that he write today. Surely racism, as well as sexism and the other forms of prejudice that Paul does name, is an affront to the unity of the Christian family. In the case of Galatians 3:28, the author's principle is spelled out; in other passages its discovery may require careful reading and a knowledge of the writer's cultural setting. By using a method of procedure such as this, however, one can at the same time represent accurately the thoughts of the original author without imposing his own views on them, while at the same time applying the biblical teachings to one's present situation so that the message of the Bible may be clearly heard today.

---

50. See F. M. Snowden, Jr., "Blacks, Early Christianity and," in the supplementary volume to the *Interpreter's Dictionary of the Bible,* pp. 111–112.

4. The reader should not attempt to interpret the Bible in isolation from the communities of learning and of faith which have preceded him. A middle course is to be steered between total dependence on the guidance of others as though one were incapable of reading profitably by oneself, and total independence of others as though all the study and prayer of previous readers had profited nothing. There are three sorts of communities with which the reader is advised to remain in communication. The first is the community of biblical scholarship. Although even the beginning reader can benefit from his own study of the Bible, there are none so far advanced that they have nothing to learn from others. Even the most experienced specialists learn from one another at professional conferences and from those who preceded them in their disciplines. It is unlikely that the less-specialized reader would be well advised to choose to dispense with the things which others have learned.

This is, of course, not to imply that one can draw no conclusions from reading the Bible without first referring to the consensus of modern scholars. It is rather that, having reached one's own tentative conclusions, it is often useful to see how other, more experienced interpreters have understood the passage at hand. The critical issue is not whether these can "prove" or "disprove" one's own thought, but whether the facts and reasoning employed by others who have studied the text in greater depth might from time to time give the reader cause to revise some of the conclusions to which he or she had initially been inclined. One need not agree with what others conclude; it is somewhat arrogant, however, to dismiss the work of those who have gone before without entertaining the possibility that anything of value could be learned from what they discovered. Especially where a check indicates that considerable uncertainty exists among experienced scholars concerning an interpretative issue, the reader is advised to exercise caution. In particular, it is appropriate to recall at this point the cautions which were expressed in the preceding chapters about the theological or ethical interpretation of passages where, because of translational or textual difficulties, the author's intended meaning is not clear. One is on thin ice in such cases, and is advised to place no more weight on them than they will bear.

In addition to holding membership (however junior) in the community of scholars, the Christian reader of the Bible is also a member of the community of faith. The major contours of biblical theology have already been charted by earlier generations of Christian thinkers. It is typical of the sort of thinking which is found in sects and cults, however, to ignore the insights of earlier religious thinkers and to assume that one's own interpretative idiosyncrasies represent—discovered/revealed at long last!—the essential truth which was hidden from all those who had labored over the Scriptures before.[51] Of course, new perspectives and insights do occur from time to time, and many of these have been helpful in illuminating aspects of the Christian faith. What is characteristic of sectarian thinking, however, is not the fact of such insights, but the conception that, without them, something essential to Christianity itself has been missed.[52]

There are three ways by which the reader of the Bible can benefit from recognizing himself as a part of the larger and older Christian community. The first is that there is often guidance available in making use of the passage which one may be reading. It has often been the case that readers have been assisted in a theological, ethical, or devotional application of a passage by reading what some other Christian thinker has written about it. The second, and perhaps more valuable, benefit which one may receive from the larger Christian community is a setting in which to place his own reading of the Bible. It can seem, especially to the beginning reader, that an insight gained from one's study of the Bible is one's alone. A realization that others may have reached the same conclusions may serve to confirm the value of that insight. This

---

51. In earlier, more polemical days of interchurch relationships, Catholics accused Protestants of just this sort of thinking: "The true Gospel, you Protestants believe, was taught by Jesus and immediately forgotten, and was only rediscovered some fifteen hundred years later by Martin Luther." This caricature, it is now recognized, was incorrect on two grounds: (1) the early Protestants did not believe that theirs was newly-found truth, but that it had always been recognized as the Gospel, and quoted many, especially of the Church Fathers, in support of this claim; (2) the Protestant way of seeing things was in their eyes necessary to the full being or purity of the Church, but not to its very existence, as though no pre-Reformation believers could have been Christians.

52. As an example, E. J. Carnell, a Protestant evangelical, accuses some of his fellow evangelicals of sectarian thinking when such matters as a particular view of the second coming of Jesus are treated as though they were essential to Christianity itself, in *The Case for Orthodox Theology* (Philadelphia: Westminster, 1959), pp. 113–119.

confirmation, of course, need not detract from the rewarding sense of having made what was for him or her a fresh discovery. Finally, if one is an active participant in the life and study of a particular church, the practical insights gained from reading the Bible may be of use to others as well. By one's willingness to share one's learnings with others, one can participate in the teaching ministry of the whole Christian community.

A third sort of membership that most readers of the Bible will have is in a particular branch of the larger Christian community. Few people can be Christians-in-general; most will have chosen to join or to remain within a particular theological family within the larger whole. By such an affiliation, one will have adopted a set of religious mentors as well as a group of Christian colleagues. The benefits of reading the Bible within the smaller circle of a particular Christian tradition will be similar to those discussed above in connection with the larger community. These benefits, moreover, will frequently be more suited to the point of view and temperament of the individual reader. A Protestant and a Catholic may not draw the same devotional application, say, from Jesus' reference to himself as "the bread of life" in John 6:47–51; the Protestant may think of a subjective union with Christ which comes through prayer and devotion, while the Catholic will likely think of the sacrament of the Eucharist as an objective reality. The devotional needs of both, however, will be served by each. Especially for the beginning reader of the Bible who is at the same time beginning to explore Christianity as a personal way of life, to locate himself within a particular branch of the Christian family and to explore its distinctive contributions to living as a Christian may be more helpful and less confusing than to attempt a sort of in-general Christian life, the religious equivalent of the jack of all trades who has mastered none. Each of the major forms of Christianity has resources which, when utilized, will assist the less-experienced Christian not only in his reading of the Bible but in the whole of Christian thinking and living.

5

Where Do I Go From Here?

This book has been designed as an owner's manual for the new reader of the Bible, describing its features and showing how they may be used. Its first chapter discussed the contents of the Bible and how they are arranged. The next chapter described the history of biblical translation and reviewed several versions of the Bible. The chapter which followed showed how to understand and to use the various sorts of footnotes and other helps which are appended to the text of many editions of the Bible. The fourth chapter illustrated the most important methods which have been used in interpreting the Bible and offered suggestions for the theological and personal use of the Bible by the beginning reader.

With the completion of the preceding chapter, the goal for which this book was written has been reached: to give the beginning reader the basic sorts of information needed in order to start to read the Bible for himself or herself. The moment to bid farewell to the reader, however, has not yet come. Since the purpose of this book is to prepare the reader for his or her own study of the Bible, it is perhaps appropriate to offer some concluding suggestions as to what next steps in biblical study the reader might choose to take. This chapter will describe some of the avenues for further study which are available to readers of the Bible. An important feature of this chapter will be an annotated bibliography of resources, some of which might be explored by the reader as a next step in the study of the Bible. The range of possibilities is large, and possibly even unsettling. Not even the most advanced specialist, however, has mastered everything there is to know about the Bible.[1] A constructive attitude is the statement about study made by a rabbi who lived about a century after Jesus: "It is not thy part to finish the task, yet thou art not free to desist from it."[2] The purpose of the present chapter is to sort out some of the options for continuing study which exist.

Options in Continuing Biblical Study

There are several ways in which one may continue one's study of the Bible. The best choice for some readers may be to join a Bible study group. These groups, often conducted quite informally, are frequently sponsored by a church or religious organization. Protestant churches usually offer continuing education classes for adults on Sunday mornings. Catholic churches often offer Bible study classes at various times. The organization and procedure of Bible study groups differs from group to group. In some cases, each member of the group is expected to have read the passage under consideration and is offered an opportunity to comment on it. In other instances an individual, perhaps a member of the group, is designated to be the teacher, prepares a lecture in advance and delivers it to the group. A textbook is usually used in Bible study groups, although some prefer to use only the Bible itself together with the resources available to the various members. The purposes of church-related Bible study groups may vary: in addition to studying the Bible itself, many are concerned to strengthen friendships among the group members or to encourage the participants' religious devotion. Frequently members combine their studies with a period of devotional meditation or prayer. Less commonly, classes in the Bible are used by churches and related organizations as an opportunity to persuade non-members to join the supporting church. In a few cases, unscrupulous advocates of a particular religious viewpoint use this means to locate prospective converts to be approached later in a high-pressure evange-

---

1. One becomes an advanced specialist by specializing: by carving away larger and larger areas of knowledge which one will not attempt to master, in order to approach mastery of that which remains. The textual critic and the biblical historian must each consult the other for information outside their own specialized disciplines.

2. Rabbi Tarfon, quoted in Pirke Aboth 2:16, a very old portion of the Talmud. Cf. Herbert Danby, *The Mishnah* (London: Oxford University Press, 1933), p. 449.

lism effort. While this is not common among responsible religious organizations, it occurs in some quarters, and the individual seeking a Bible study group should be aware of the possibility. It is perhaps best to seek a Bible study group in a denomination with which one is already familiar in order to avoid the possibility of becoming treated as a candidate for conversion.

It has just been stated that Bible study groups often combine their studies with other devotional or religious activities. In addition, church-related Bible study groups often mirror the theological viewpoint of their sponsoring organizations. The objectivity and ecumenicity which has characterized modern biblical study among scholars has not always descended to the local congregations! The reader interested in the objective study of the Bible rather than only in its theological and devotional application might be better advised to investigate courses in the Bible at a local college. An obvious source for such classes is the church-related college. Almost all denominational institutions offer biblical courses which are open to members of the community who are not seeking a degree. In most instances, the quality of instruction, of scholarly objectivity, and of ecumenical sensitivity found in such classes will be superior to that of church-related Bible study groups. A second source for courses in the Bible is the public university or community college. An increasing number of public institutions offer classes in biblical topics. The state university in which I teach has courses entitled "Introduction to the Bible" and "How to Study the Bible," as well as more advanced classes in the Old and New Testaments. Some public universities have full major programs in religious studies; many others offer occasional courses in biblical matters. A final source of courses in the Bible might be a seminary related to one's own or another denomination. Students in seminaries study the Bible as part of their preparation for the pastoral ministry. Since many seminarians enter with little formal training in the Bible, introductory courses are often offered, and these are often open to interested laypersons.

A third way of continuing one's study of the Bible is to engage in a course of self-directed study. A large number of books on biblical topics are published annually by both religious and secular publishers; many of these would be useful to the continuing student of the Bible. In general, most of the books published by the larger and better-known denominational and commercial presses represent the mainstream of contemporary biblical scholarship.[3] Books from smaller, out-of-the-way publishers or which have been published privately by their authors are sometimes works which have been rejected by knowledgeable reviewers employed by the larger presses; these should be used with caution. Useful books may be found in most commercial bookstores; religion is a popular field among the general public. These outlets, however, will usually not stock the more specialized books among those described in the bibliography below. For these, the reader might investigate a religious bookstore which will either have the desired works in stock or be able to order them quickly. The present writer prefers to be able to examine a book at least briefly before committing himself to its purchase, however, and the reader might wish to do the same. A remaining source of books is the library. Larger public libraries often have good holdings in biblical studies; the same is true of many college and university libraries. Churches sometimes have libraries which circulate books among their members. Sadly, one must eventually return books to their home libraries, but these remain a source to be explored. Libraries often have books which are out of print, and they provide a way by which books in print may be examined before being purchased.

Resources: An Annotated Bibliography

The writer of Ecclesiastes observed wearily over two millennia ago that "of making many books there is no end" (12:12); and this was written before the invention of the printing press! A vast number of books on the Bible are available in bookstores and in libraries. Some of these will not be useful for the beginning student of the Bible; many are technical and addressed to more specialized scholars. A smaller number

---

3. Many Protestant denominations have sponsored publishing houses. Among these are Broadman Press (Baptist), John Knox Press and Westminster Press (both Presbyterian), Abingdon Press (Methodist), Fortress Press and Augsburg Publishing House (both Lutheran), and Seabury Press (Episcopalian). Two other Protestant-oriented publishers are Eerdmans Publishing Company and Zondervan Publishing House; their books are often aimed toward evangelical readers. Several publishers print books of a Catholic orientation; only two examples are Orbis Books and the Paulist/Newman Press.

have substantive errors of fact or are out of date. The following is intended as a guide for the reader of the present work who is looking for resources to continue his study of the Bible. These books are of varying levels of difficulty, but all should be within reach of the reader who has completed the present volume. They are arranged topically.

Study Bibles. A handy resource for studying the Bible is an edition which provides introductory materials and other notes to assist the reader. Two important study Bibles are *The New Oxford Annotated Bible, with the Apocrypha* (New York: Oxford University Press, 1977), and *The New English Bible with the Apocrypha: Oxford Study Edition* (New York: Oxford University Press, 1976). The former is based on the Revised Standard Version, the latter on the New English Bible. The Revised Standard Version is perhaps to be preferred for continuing study since this is the version which is most frequently cited and used by the authors of secondary resources such as those discussed below.

Commentaries. There exists a practical limit to the amount of information which can be printed in the margins and at the foot of pages in a study Bible. For more detailed information one must go to a commentary. Commentaries are arranged according to the biblical sequence and can be read along with the passage itself. Several distinctive kinds of commentaries exist. Some commentaries are designed to assist in the preparations of sermons and homilies based on the text; these often include illustrative anecdotes and devotional applications, but are usually of little use in investigating the meaning of biblical text itself. A more useful sort of commentary provides historical, linguistic, and cultural information necessary for understanding the passage. A conveniently-sized commentary of this type is *The Interpreter's One-Volume Commentary on the Bible* (Nashville: Abingdon, 1971). This 1,386-page work, written by an interdenominational group of contributors, provides commentary on the entire Bible (including the deuterocanonical books) together with a number of articles of interest to the student of the Scriptures. (This work should not be confused with the multi-volume *Interpreter's Bible* from the same publisher. The latter combines information similar to that of the *One-Volume Commentary* with a set of homiletical notes and the text of the King James and Revised Standard Versions. The reader will find only the first of these contents useful, and there is no sense in buying a more expensive and cumbersome work than one needs.) A contemporary commentary which will be of special interest to Catholics is the *Jerome Biblical Commentary* (Englewood Cliffs, New Jersey: Prentice-Hall, 1969). Many other commentaries exist; the reader would be advised to examine a possible purchase to be sure his interests coincide with those of the writers before committing his money.

Dictionaries and Other Helps with Words. A standard resource for the study of the Bible is the five-volume *Interpreter's Dictionary of the Bible* (Nashville: Abingdon, 1962; supplementary volume 1976). Its usefulness to the reader of the Bible may be observed by the number of times it has been cited in the notes to this volume; together with copies of the Bible itself and English-language dictionaries, the *Interpreter's Dictionary of the Bible* is always kept in easy reach of my working desk. This work is an encyclopedia of biblical knowledge, including articles on all proper names and on most of the important terms found in the Bible. An international group of Protestant, Catholic, and Jewish scholars contributed to this project. The articles are intended to summarize succinctly what is known about each of the subjects and to offer basic information sought by the beginning reader as well as more detailed discussions needed by the advanced student. A valuable assistance to the scholar who consults this work is the bibliography included in each article. A supplementary volume, cross-indexed to the original four volumes, was published in 1976 and updates many of the original articles. This work, although not inexpensive, is in my view the most important resource a Bible student can own along with the Bible itself. Smaller and less expensive dictionaries also exist. Among these is the *New Westminster Dictionary of the Bible* (Philadelphia: Westminster, 1970). This one-volume work, although not encyclopedic, will be of use in defining key biblical terms. A similar volume is the *New Bible Dictionary* (Grand Rapids: Eerdmans, 1972), which was written by a group of evangelical Protestant scholars. This work takes a consistently conservative position on critical matters, in my view, even when the evidence might incline one otherwise. It is popular in evangelical circles and may be useful to readers who share its theological orientation.

A quite different sort of guide to the vocabulary of the Bible is a concordance. This book, in its exhaustive forms, is a complete index to every word in the Bible, arranged alphabetically and briefly indicating the context in which it appears. Smaller and less useful versions are found in some Bibles. Its most common use is in locating a passage which the reader can remember but cannot find. One looks up a key word, scans for the remembered phrase in which that word appears, and finds the reference. A second, more technical use is to locate every occurrence of a biblical term in order to study its development and meaning throughout the Bible. The classical concordances are *Cruden's Concordance* (originally published in 1737; available from several publishers), *Strong's Exhaustive Concordance of the Bible* (Nashville, Thomas Nelson, 1977), and *Young's Analytical Concordance to the Bible* (Grand Rapids, Eerdmans, 1955). These are not all of the same quality.[4] *Strong's* and *Young's* concordances can allow the reader who has mastered their systems of notation to access the uses of each word in the original biblical languages, regardless of the ways by which they were translated into English. All three are based on the classic King James Version. A more recent concordance is *An Analytical Concordance to the Revised Standard Version of the New Testament* by Clinton Morrison (Philadelphia: Westminster, 1979). This work has several important technical features which will make it useful to scholars. It is, however, expensive and limited to the New Testament. Non-specialized readers would perhaps be better advised to purchase *Strong's* or *Young's* if they want to own a concordance. While each of the latter has its partisans, there is little reason to prefer one over the other, and the decision which to buy might as well be based on price as any other factor.

A final work which may be mentioned among aids to understanding the vocabulary of the Bible is Edward W. Goodrick's *Do It Yourself Hebrew and Greek* (Grand Rapids, Michigan: Zondervan; Portland, Oregon: Multnomah Press, 1980). This volume is a workbook which introduces its reader to a sufficient knowledge of Greek and Hebrew orthography and grammar to enable him to use the standard dictionaries, commentaries, and other resources which are normally inacces-

---

4. A saying once went, "*Young's* for the young, *Strong's* for the strong, and *Cruden's* for the crude." The writer, who is not quite young, uses *Young's* nevertheless.

sible to those who do not know the biblical languages. Chapter 6 of this book describes in detail how to use a concordance to locate each English occurrence of a word in the original language. (Goodrick is clear that this book is not a substitute for language study by the advanced student: he repeatedly calls his approach the "low road" and warns his readers of its limitations.) The book is not without its flaws: its treatment of Hebrew is inadequate, and its orientation is perhaps too exclusively toward an evangelical readership. In general, however, it serves a useful purpose and will assist those who wish to begin to use some of the more advanced linguistic tools in their study of the Bible.

Introductions to Biblical Culture and History. One of the most important contributions of recent historical studies has been to underscore the necessity of an approach to the Bible which takes seriously its historical and cultural context. A knowledge of the times out of which the biblical writings have come is essential to the serious reader of the Bible. An excellent resource for the reader of the Old Testament is John Bright's *A History of Israel* (Philadelphia: Westminster, 1981). This volume of over five hundred pages is a new revised edition incorporating many of the new discoveries which have been made since the book was first issued in 1959. *A History of Israel* describes the historical, political, and cultural setting of the ancient Hebrews and traces their history from their beginnings to the re-establishment of an independent state of Judah in the middle of the second century B.C. There are many books which seek to place the New Testament in its historical setting. Of these, the two which follow may be of interest to the continuing student: Samuel Sandmel's *The First Christian Century in Judaism and Christianity* (New York: Oxford, 1969) and Hans Conzelmann's *History of Primitive Christianity* (Nashville: Abingdon, 1973). Sandmel's book is an excellent introduction to the Jewish background of early Christianity. Sandmel is a careful scholar who distinguishes clearly between what can be known about the setting of early Christianity and what cannot. His book is particularly useful for observing the diversity which existed in first century Judaism; the latter was not, as is often thought, a rigid system of religious orthodoxy. Conzelmann's *History* complements Sandmel's work nicely: Sandmel describes the setting of early Christianity, and Conzelmann narrates its development to the end of the first century. Either or both of these books would be useful for the reader of the New Testament.

Several other resources may be mentioned more briefly. The setting of the events of the Bible is geographical as well as historical, and a set of maps is often useful to the reader. I use the *Oxford Bible Atlas* (London: Oxford, 1962). Others, equally useful, are available. A final and rather more effortless way of becoming aware of the cultural setting of portions of the Bible is to read James Michener's historical novel, *The Source* (New York: Random House, 1965). This book combines a narrative about modern archaeologists with a series of short stories about the origins of the artifacts which they discover. Although this book is a work of fiction, the cultural settings Michener describes are generally accurate. Stories of interest to readers of the Bible are "The Old Man and His God" (describing the patriarchal period), "The Hoopoe Bird" (the reign of King David), "The Voice of Gomer" (the prophets and the exile), "In the Gymnasium" (the period of Greek rule and the Maccabees), "The King of the Jews" (Herod), and "Yigal and His Three Generals" (the events leading to the Jewish war against Rome of 66–74 A.D.).

Biblical Introductions. An "introduction" is a special kind of resource for the reader of the Bible. In contrast to a commentary, which discusses particular passages, and a book of history, which describes the setting of a portion of the Bible, an introduction is concerned with the biblical writing itself. Typically, an introduction seeks to give the background information needed to understand a particular book of the Bible, including such matters as an outline of its contents, its author and date of composition, and the situation of its original readers. Since many of the biblical writings were originally letters addressed to a particular group of readers, information of this sort is often needed in order to understand the writing fully. The most technical introductions summarize the current state of biblical scholarship, and are usually consulted by specialists in the course of research. The reader of the present volume is more likely to consult an introduction written for the nonspecialist, which will make use of current research but which will not burden the reader with the technical details required only by the scholar. A number of books of this sort have been written; among them is Samuel Sandmel's introduction to the Old Testament, entitled *The Hebrew Scriptures* (New York: Oxford, 1978) and Oscar Cullmann's *The New Testament: An Introduction for the General Reader* (Philadelphia: Westminster, 1968). Both of these are available in paperback, and each is written for the non-specialist. Either or both of these volumes would be an appropriate "next step" reading for the person who has finished the present work.

Introductions to Biblical Scholarship. To write books such as those described in the preceding paragraphs requires that an author be aware of much of modern biblical scholarship so that he can make use of its discoveries in the course of his writing. The author is somewhat like the cook who selects from a number of possible ingredients the things that will go into the prepared meal. But sometimes one wants not only to sample the cuisine, but to get a look into the kitchen itself. Modern scholarship, as we have seen, involves a number of distinctive disciplines, and no scholars have mastered them all. It is possible, however, to become aware of some of the procedures of modern research by exploring one or more of the books described below.

The following books differ somewhat in terms of their intended readership. Some are intended to introduce modern biblical studies to the general reader, while others describe the methods in greater detail for the more advanced student. Among the books designed for the beginning student of the Bible is Brian E. Beck's *Reading the New Testament Today* (Atlanta: John Knox, 1978). This book illustrates the techniques of textual, source, redaction, and form criticism, and shows how they are applied to biblical passages. This work may be the best general introduction to modern methods of biblical scholarship for the reader of the present book. Two other books introduce particular disciplines in an equally non-technical manner. These are Eugene Nida's *Good News for Everyone* (Waco, Texas: Word Books, 1977), which discusses matters of biblical translation, and Gerhard Lohfink's *The Bible: Now I Get It!* (Garden City, New York: Doubleday, 1979), which introduces the techniques of form criticism. The latter is an especially well-written work which includes analyses of such things as recipes, jokes, and a "letter to Aunt Fanny" in presenting the study of fixed forms which are found in the Bible. The reader interested in a more technical history of modern research in the Bible might wish to read Ronald E. Clements' *One Hundred Years of Old Testament Interpretation* (Philadelphia: Westminster, 1976) or Stephen Neill's *The Interpretation of the New Testament: 1861–1961* (Oxford: Oxford University Press, 1966).

On a somewhat more advanced level, a very useful set of introductions to biblical scholarship is the Guides to Biblical Scholarship series of small books published by Fortress Press in Philadelphia. The books of this series include: Edgar V. McKnight's *What Is Form Criticism?* (1969), Norman Perrin's *What Is Redaction Criticism?* (1969), Dan O. Via's *Literary Criticism of the New Testament* (1970), Norman Habel's *Literary Criticism of the Old Testament* (1971), Gene M. Tucker's *Form Criticism of the Old Testament* (1971), Walter E. Rast's *Tradition History and the Old Testament* (1972), William G. Doty's *Letters in Primitive Christianity* (1973), Ralph W. Klein's *Textual Criticism of the Old Testament* (1974), Edgar Krentz's *The Historical-Critical Method* (1975), J. Maxwell Miller's *The Old Testament and the Historian* (1976), Daniel Patte's *What Is Structural Exegesis?* (1976), and David Robertson's *The Old Testament and the Literary Critic* (1977). These books typically include a discussion of the origins of the method under consideration and illustrations of its use.

Guides to the Theological Use of the Bible. The development of Christian theology has been closely tied to the history of the interpretation of the Bible. A concise description of the latter is Robert M. Grant's *A Short History of the Interpretation of the Bible* (New York: Macmillan, 1963). In this small book, which has unfortunately gone out of print, the author narrates the development of methods of interpretation from the beginnings of Christianity to the Protestant Reformation, and of the history of biblical studies in Protestantism and in Catholicism to the present. Although Grant frequently provides more detail and more names than the reader of the present book may want, his work will interest those who wish to explore more deeply the matters discussed in the previous chapter. Another, more specialized history of the interpretation of the Bible is *The Authority and Interpretation of the Bible: An Historical Approach,* by Jack B. Rogers and Donald K. McKim (San Francisco: Harper and Row, 1979). This book describes the history of biblical interpretation in Protestantism. Of particular interest for many readers will be the authors' discussions of the origins of doctrines of biblical inerrancy and of recent Protestant interpretations of the Bible.

Perhaps a result of the Protestant conviction that the essential teachings of the Bible can be understood by everyone is that most popular-level guides to the interpretation of the Bible have been written by and for Protestants. A typical example is A. Berkeley Mickelsen's *Interpreting the Bible* (Grand Rapids: Eerdmans, 1963). Mickelsen's book is a text in biblical exegesis for the interpreter who is not a professional scholar. Asserting as general interpretative principles that one should understand a biblical passage in its context, with attention to its linguistic and grammatical details, and in terms of its historical setting, the author instructs the reader in interpreting biblical figures of speech, symbols, and poetry, and in applying the Bible to theology, ethics, and devotion. Mickelsen is conversant with contemporary scholarship, although his own views are to the conservative side of its mainstream. The more advanced student would benefit from working through this book.

Several introductions to the theology of the Bible exist. An important example is Alan Richardson's *An Introduction to the Theology of the New Testament* (Naperville, Illinois: Allenson, 1958). This book is a discussion of the major themes in New Testament theology, including the kingdom of God, Christ, the Church, Christian ministry, and the sacraments. Richardson's book is scholarly and well-written. He often quotes a word or phrase from the Greek of the New Testament; these can usually be ignored by the reader who does not know that language.

The Next Step and the Step After That

The first four chapters of this book were addressed to the beginning reader of the Bible, and were written to assist in reading the Bible in a way which is both informed and personally satisfying. The present chapter has assumed that the readers of this book may wish to continue their study of the Bible after finishing the present volume, and has suggested a number of options for pursuing one's study. One final question may be asked: Suppose the present book has served as an appetizer, not just for a further taste, but for a regular diet—what might one do, not only as one's next step, but as a program of continued biblical learning beyond that? Many of the suggestions made earlier in this chapter, of course, will apply as well to long-term interests as to one's next immediate steps. One can take a course, and then another; one can read a book, and then study several more.

The reader who anticipates a continuing interest in biblical studies may desire more specific suggestions than "more of the same." A first suggestion is that some sort of guidance is usually helpful. The reader who has not completed college may consider becoming a religious studies major and taking biblical courses as part of his academic program. (Such a choice need not lead to unemployment after graduation; religious studies, like English, philosophy, and psychology, is a "liberal arts" field often valued by employers seeking intelligent and trainable personnel.) Other readers might inquire about programs of directed study available from denominational colleges or seminaries. Several such schools offer syllabi and other guides for continuing education which can be mailed to those who are interested in biblical and related studies. A third option may be to subscribe to one of the several journals that publish serious but not overly-technical articles in the field. One such journal is *Biblical Archaeologist,* published in Chico, California, by Scholars Press for the American Schools of Oriental Research. This journal seeks to inform the non-specialized reader of current developments in research into biblical history. Articles on biblical topics are also often found in denominational and other religious journals.

A second suggestion is offered especially to the religious reader of the Bible: an important part of one's own learning can be to teach others. Professionals and other teachers agree that there is little that will stimulate one's own careful study and critical reflection more than the responsibility of teaching what one has learned to others. Most churches have ongoing programs of education for adults and for younger people; most of these are continuously on the lookout for teachers. That someone learns to read the Bible intelligently and to interpret it carefully, using the insights of modern research, and that he or she then begins to teach others is beyond a doubt a contribution to those who are taught; it is also a valuable experience for the one who teaches. In the view of the Christian community, the learning Church and the teaching Church minister in Christ's name to each other.